TypeScript for Blockchain

Unlock the full Potential of TypeScript
in Web3 Development

Adriam Miller

1

Discover Other Books in the Series

Disclaimer

The information provided in *"TypeScript for Blockchain: Unlock the Full Potential of TypeScript in Web3 Development"* by **Adriam Miller** is for educational and informational purposes only.

This Book is designed to provide insights into TypeScript programming and its applications in blockchain and Web3 development.

Introduction

The world of blockchain is evolving at an unprecedented pace, and with it comes the demand for powerful, scalable, and secure applications. Whether you're a developer looking to transition into Web3 or an experienced programmer seeking to optimize your workflow, TypeScript is the game-changer you've been waiting for.

In the ever-expanding blockchain ecosystem, writing clean, maintainable, and bug-free code is not just a preference—it's a necessity. Smart contracts, decentralized applications (dApps), and Web3 integrations demand precision, security, and efficiency. This is where TypeScript shines. With its static typing, advanced tooling, and developer-friendly features, TypeScript empowers you to build robust blockchain solutions with confidence—minimizing errors while maximizing productivity.

This Book, *TypeScript for Blockchain: Unlock the Full Potential of TypeScript in Web3 Development,* is your ultimate guide to mastering TypeScript in the Web3 space. From the fundamentals of TypeScript to building real-world blockchain applications, this book takes you through step-by-step implementations, best practices, and powerful coding techniques that will set you apart in the industry.

Chapter 1: Getting Started with TypeScript

With the proliferation of decentralized applications, smart contracts, and various blockchain protocols, developers are constantly seeking tools that can enhance their productivity while ensuring code reliability and maintainability. Among the array of programming languages available, TypeScript has emerged as a leading choice for blockchain development. This chapter aims to provide an overview of TypeScript and its significance in the context of blockchain technology.

1.1 What is TypeScript?

TypeScript is an open-source programming language developed and maintained by Microsoft. It is a superset of JavaScript, which means that any valid JavaScript code is also valid TypeScript code. TypeScript introduces static typing, which allows developers to explicitly define data types, thereby enhancing code quality and reducing the likelihood of runtime errors. This feature becomes particularly valuable in large- scale projects, where managing complex codebases can be a daunting task.

Key Features of TypeScript

Static Typing: One of the most significant advantages of TypeScript is its static type system. By allowing developers to define types for variables, function parameters, and return values, TypeScript helps catch errors during development rather than at runtime.

Enhanced IDE Support: TypeScript is designed with modern development tools in mind. Most Integrated Development Environments (IDEs) and text editors provide features like autocompletion, refactoring, and real-time type checking, which enhance developer efficiency.

Modern JavaScript Features: TypeScript supports the latest JavaScript features, allowing developers to leverage advancements such as async/await, destructuring, and more, often before they are fully implemented in JavaScript engines.

Interoperability with JavaScript: Since TypeScript is a superset of JavaScript, developers can incrementally adopt it in existing JavaScript projects. This allows teams to gradually introduce TypeScript's benefits without needing a complete rewrite of their codebase.

1.2 The Relevance of TypeScript in Blockchain Development

The blockchain landscape encompasses diverse applications, including cryptocurrencies, supply chain management, decentralized finance (DeFi), and non-fungible tokens (NFTs). As the complexity of blockchain applications grows, the need for robust programming languages that can handle intricate logic becomes increasingly critical. Here is why TypeScript stands out in blockchain development:

1.2.1 Improved Code Quality and Developer Productivity

Blockchain projects often involve handling sensitive data and managing financial transactions, where security is paramount. The static typing feature of TypeScript helps to enforce stricter type checks, enabling developers to identify potential issues early in the development cycle.

This leads to fewer bugs and a more secure codebase.

1.2.2 Scalability and Maintainability

As blockchain applications grow in size and complexity, maintaining the code becomes challenging. TypeScript's type system helps developers write self-documenting code, making it easier for teams to collaborate and understand each other's code. This maintainability is particularly important in blockchain environments, where projects often have long lifecycles and require ongoing updates.

1.2.3 Compatibility with Popular Frameworks and Libraries

TypeScript has gained popularity in the blockchain community partly due to its compatibility with various frameworks and libraries. For instance, developers can use TypeScript with libraries like ethers.js and web3.js, which provide essential functionality for interacting with blockchain networks. Moreover, frameworks like Hardhat and Truffle support TypeScript, allowing developers to write, deploy, and test smart contracts more efficiently.

1.3 Setting the Stage for This Book

Throughout this book, we will explore how TypeScript can be effectively utilized in the context of blockchain development. From foundational concepts to advanced techniques, we will cover a range of topics including:

Setting up a TypeScript development environment for blockchain projects

Understanding smart contract development with TypeScript

Utilizing TypeScript with popular blockchain libraries

Best practices for testing and deploying TypeScript-based smart contracts

Real-world case studies of successful TypeScript blockchain projects

By the end of this book, readers will have a comprehensive understanding of how to leverage TypeScript in their blockchain projects, enhancing their ability to build secure, maintainable, and scalable applications.

As blockchain technology continues to mature, the demand for reliable and efficient development tools has never been greater. TypeScript, with its powerful features and strong community support, has positioned itself as an invaluable asset for blockchain developers. By embracing TypeScript, developers can improve the quality of their code, streamline their workflows, and ultimately deliver better solutions in the rapidly- evolving blockchain landscape.

Understanding TypeScript: Features & Benefits

TypeScript is rapidly gaining traction as a superset of JavaScript that is designed for development on large-scale applications. It enhances JavaScript by adding static typing, interfaces, and other features that aim to improve the development experience and the robustness of applications. In this chapter, we will explore the key features of TypeScript and the benefits it brings to developers and teams.

1. What is TypeScript?

TypeScript is an open-source programming language developed by Microsoft. Introduced in 2012, TypeScript builds on JavaScript, adding optional static typing and other features that allow developers to catch errors early in the development process, improve code readability, and enhance teamwork on larger projects.

One of TypeScript's primary goals is to provide developers with a more structured language while maintaining compatibility with existing JavaScript code. This means that any valid JavaScript code is also valid TypeScript code, allowing for a smooth transition for developers who are accustomed to working in JavaScript.

2. Key Features of TypeScript ### 2.1 Static Typing

One of the most notable features of TypeScript is its optional static typing system. By defining variable types, function parameters, and return types, developers can catch type-related errors at compile time rather than at runtime. This leads to fewer bugs and improves overall code quality. For instance:

```typescript
function greet(name: string): string { return `Hello, ${name}`;
}
// Example of a type error
greet(42); // This will raise a compile-time error
```

2.2 Interfaces

TypeScript supports the creation of interfaces, which allow developers to define the structure of an object. This feature promotes better organization of code and ensures that objects adhere to specific formats, making it easier to work collaboratively.

```typescript
interface Person {

name: string; age: number;

}

function printPerson(person: Person) {

console.log(`Name: ${person.name}, Age: ${person.age}`);

}
```

2.3 Enhanced Code Navigation

TypeScript provides advanced tools for code navigation, such as autocompletion, refactoring support, and better code organization. This improves the developer experience, as it allows developers to understand and manipulate the codebase more effectively. Development environments like Visual Studio Code offer rich support, enabling features like Go to Definition and Find All References.

2.4 Type Inference

While TypeScript is statically typed, it also includes a powerful type inference system. This means that TypeScript can automatically determine the type of a variable based on its initial value, which reduces the need for explicit type annotations and enhances code conciseness.

```typescript
let count = 10; // TypeScript infers 'count' as 'number'
count = 'twenty'; // This will raise an error
```

2.5 Decorators

TypeScript introduces decorator syntax, which allows developers to annotate and modify classes and methods. This is particularly useful in frameworks like Angular, where decorators are used to enhance components and services.

2.6 Genuine Object-Oriented Features

TypeScript incorporates features from modern object-oriented programming languages, such as classes, inheritance, and access modifiers (public, private, and protected). These features allow developers to write more modular and maintainable code.

3. Benefits of Using TypeScript

3.1 Improved Code Quality and Safety

By catching errors at compile-time, TypeScript significantly reduces the likelihood of runtime errors, leading to better application stability. The use of types ensures that the code adheres to defined contracts, thus enhancing maintainability.

3.2 Better Developer Experience

Tools that support TypeScript enable developers to take advantage of features like autocompletion, inline documentation, and real-time error reporting. This leads to a smoother development experience with increased productivity.

3.3 Enhanced Collaboration

In team environments, TypeScript enables better collaboration by providing a clear structure for code. With type annotations and interfaces, team members can better understand the expected input and output of functions and classes, reducing miscommunication.

3.4 Continuous Growth and Support

As TypeScript continues to evolve, a growing community actively contributes to its development, ensuring that it keeps pace with the latest JavaScript features and best practices. The backing from Microsoft also provides ongoing resources and support for TypeScript users.

3.5 Compatibility with JavaScript

As a superset of JavaScript, TypeScript is inherently compatible with all JavaScript libraries and frameworks. This means that developers can gradually adopt TypeScript in their existing projects, allowing for a low-risk transition.

By introducing optional static typing, enhanced code navigation, and improved collaboration tools, TypeScript not only enhances the developer experience but also produces more reliable and maintainable code. As the demand for scalable applications continues to grow, TypeScript's popularity is likely to keep soaring, establishing it as a mainstay in the toolkits of developers worldwide.

Setting Up a TypeScript Development Environment

In this chapter, we will walk through the necessary steps to set up a TypeScript development environment, enabling you to harness the full power of this robust language.

1. Prerequisites

Before diving into the setup process, ensure that you have the following prerequisites:

Node.js: TypeScript relies on Node.js for package management via npm (Node Package Manager). If Node.js is not already installed, download it from the [official Node.js website](https://nodejs.org) and follow the installation instructions for your operating system.

A Code Editor: While you can write TypeScript in any text editor, using a dedicated code editor with TypeScript support will enhance your productivity. Popular choices include Visual Studio Code, Atom, Sublime Text, and WebStorm.

Installation Verification

To verify the installation of Node.js and npm, you can run the following commands in your terminal:

```bash
node -v npm -v
```

Both commands should return the version numbers of Node.js and npm, confirming successful installation. ## 2. Creating a New Project

With your prerequisites in place, the next step is to create a new directory for your project. Open your terminal and run the following commands:

```bash
```

```bash
mkdir my-typescript-project cd my-typescript-project
```

Initializing the Project

Once inside your new project directory, you need to initialize it as a Node.js project. This creates a

`package.json` file, which will manage your project dependencies. Use the following command:

```bash
bash npm init -y
```

The `-y` flag will automatically accept the default settings, creating a `package.json` file with basic configurations.

3. Installing TypeScript

Now that we have a basic project set up, it's time to install TypeScript. To install TypeScript as a development dependency, run:

```bash
```

```bash
npm install typescript --save-dev
```

This command downloads the TypeScript package and adds it to the `devDependencies` in your

`package.json`.

17

Setting Up the TypeScript Configuration File

Next, we will set up a configuration file that allows TypeScript to compile your `.ts` files. To create a `tsconfig.json` file, run:

```bash
npx tsc --init
```

This command generates a `tsconfig.json` file with default settings. You can customize it according to your project's needs. Here's an example configuration to get you started:

```json
{
"compilerOptions": { "target": "es6", "module": "commonjs", "strict": true, "esModuleInterop": true, "skipLibCheck": true,

"forceConsistentCasingInFileNames": true, "outDir": "./dist"
},
"include": ["src/**/*"],
"exclude": ["node_modules", "**/*.spec.ts"]
}
```

Understanding the Configuration

compilerOptions: Contains settings that influence how TypeScript compiles the code.

`target`: Specifies the ECMAScript version to compile down to.

`module`: Determines the module system used.

`strict`: Enables all strict type-checking options.

`esModuleInterop`: Ensures compatibility with ES modules.

`outDir`: The directory where the compiled JavaScript files will be placed.

include: Specifies the files/directories that should be included during the compilation.

exclude: Lists files and directories to be excluded from the compilation. ## 4. Writing Your First TypeScript File

With your environment set up and your configuration in place, it's time to write your first TypeScript file. Create a new directory called `src`:

```bash
mkdir src
```

Inside the `src` directory, create a file named `index.ts`:

```typescript
// src/index.ts

const greeting: string = "Hello, TypeScript!";
console.log(greeting);
```

5. Compiling TypeScript

Now that you have a TypeScript file ready, let's compile it to JavaScript. Use the following command:

```bash npx tsc
```

This command will read your `tsconfig.json` file and compile all TypeScript files found in the `src` directory into JavaScript, placing the output files into the `dist` directory as specified.

6. Running Your Application

You can run your compiled JavaScript file using Node.js. Execute the following command:

```bash
node dist/index.js
```

If everything is set up correctly, the output will be:

```plaintext
Hello, TypeScript!
```

7. Adding Type Definitions

As your TypeScript application grows, you may want to use external libraries. To get type definitions for popular libraries, you can use npm to install the `@types` packages. For example, if you want to use Express, you would run:

```bash
npm install express @types/express --save
```

This command installs the Express library along with its

type definitions, allowing TypeScript to understand the library's structure.

You have successfully set up a TypeScript development environment. You now have a TypeScript compiler configured, a basic project structure established, and an understanding of how to write and compile TypeScript code. As you continue your journey into TypeScript, you will discover its many features, such as interfaces, generics, and advanced type manipulations, which empower you to write clean and efficient code.

Chapter 2: TypeScript Fundamentals for Blockchain Development

In this chapter, we will explore the fundamental concepts of TypeScript and how they apply to blockchain development.

2.1 What is TypeScript?

TypeScript is a superset of JavaScript that adds optional static typing to the language. Developed and maintained by Microsoft, TypeScript enables developers to catch errors during the development phase instead of at runtime, thus increasing the reliability of the code. As TypeScript compiles down to plain JavaScript, it can run in any environment where JavaScript runs, including web browsers and Node.js.

2.1.1 Key Features of TypeScript

Static Typing: This feature allows developers to define the types of variables, function parameters, and return values. Type checking during the development phase aids in reducing runtime errors and promotes code clarity.

Interfaces: TypeScript introduces interfaces, which allow developers to define the shape of an object. This is particularly useful for defining contract elements in blockchain systems, such as smart contracts.

Generics: Generics provide a way to create reusable components that work with any data type. This is beneficial for creating libraries and modules that can be used across various blockchain projects.

Decorators: A powerful feature for adding metadata to classes and functions, decorators can simplify the

22

development of smart contracts and API endpoints used in blockchain applications.

2.2 Setting Up a TypeScript Environment

To get started with TypeScript for blockchain development, you will first need to set up a suitable development environment. Here are the essential steps:

Install Node.js: TypeScript runs within Node.js, so it's necessary to install it first. Download the installer from the [official Node.js website](https://nodejs.org/) and follow the installation instructions.

Install TypeScript: Open your terminal (or command prompt) and run the following command:

```bash
npm install -g typescript
```

Create a TypeScript Project: You can initialize a new project by creating a folder for your blockchain application and navigating to it:

```bash
mkdir blockchain-project cd blockchain-project npm init -y
```

Set Up TypeScript Configuration: Create a `tsconfig.json` file to configure the TypeScript compiler settings:

```json
{
```

```
"compilerOptions": { "target": "es6", "module":
"commonjs", "strict": true, "esModuleInterop": true,
"skipLibCheck": true,
"forceConsistentCasingInFileNames": true
},
"include": ["src/**/*"],
"exclude": ["node_modules", "**/*.spec.ts"]
}
```

Create Your First TypeScript File: Inside your project, create a `src` folder and add an `index.ts` file. This is where you will write your TypeScript code.

```typescript
// src/index.ts
const greeting: string = "Hello, Blockchain!";
console.log(greeting);
```

Compile TypeScript to JavaScript: Run the TypeScript compiler to convert `index.ts` into `index.js`:

```bash
tsc
```

Run the Compiled JavaScript: Execute your code with Node.js:

```bash
node dist/index.js
```

```
```

2.3 Understanding Type Annotations

One of the core concepts in TypeScript is type annotations, which allow developers to specify the types of variables explicitly. For blockchain development, understanding these annotations is key, as it can help in defining complex data structures typically encountered in blockchain systems, such as transactions, blocks, and smart contract states.

```typescript
interface Transaction { id: string;

amount: number; sender: string; receiver: string; timestamp: Date;
}
const transaction: Transaction = { id: "1a2b3c",

amount: 100, sender: "0x12345", receiver: "0x67890",

timestamp: new Date(),

};
```

2.4 Building Robust Smart Contracts with TypeScript

Many blockchain platforms, such as Ethereum, allow developers to write smart contracts in languages like Solidity. However, TypeScript has emerged as a powerful alternative for building the front-end and back-end contracts of decentralized applications (dApps). By using TypeScript, developers can create a well-defined API that interacts seamlessly with smart contracts deployed on the blockchain.

Consider the following example demonstrating how to interact with a smart contract using TypeScript in a dApp:

```typescript
import { ethers } from "ethers";

import { YourSmartContract } from "./artifacts/YourSmartContract.json";

// Setting up your provider and signer

const provider = new ethers.providers.JsonRpcProvider("http://localhost:8545"); const signer = provider.getSigner();

// Initializing the contract

const contractAddress = "0xYourContractAddress";

const contract = new ethers.Contract(contractAddress, YourSmartContract.abi, signer);

// Interacting with the contract

async function transferTokens(receiver: string, amount: number) { try {

const tx = await contract.transfer(receiver, amount); await tx.wait(); // Wait for the transaction to be mined

console.log(`Successfully transferred ${amount} tokens to ${receiver}`);

} catch (error) {

console.error("Transaction failed:", error);

}

}
```

```

```

2.5 The Benefits of Using TypeScript in Blockchain

Using TypeScript in blockchain development offers numerous advantages:

Improved Code Quality: Having a strict type system helps catch common errors early in the development life cycle, resulting in fewer bugs in production.

Better Tooling: TypeScript provides rich tooling support, including intelligent code completion, navigation, and refactoring, which significantly enhances developer productivity.

Enhanced Collaboration: Clear type definitions improve code clarity, making it easier for teams to collaborate and maintain code over time.

Scalability: TypeScript scales better for larger projects, absorbing the complexities of growing codebases, which is common in blockchain applications as they evolve.

From setting up a TypeScript environment to exploring type annotations and smart contract interaction, TypeScript offers developers the tools they need to build reliable, maintainable, and scalable applications in the burgeoning blockchain space. With its static typing, enhanced tooling, and ultimate compatibility with JavaScript, TypeScript is a compelling choice for developers looking to make a significant impact in the blockchain domain.

Variables, Types, and Interfaces for Smart Contracts

TypeScript, a superset of JavaScript, has gained popularity for building smart contracts due to its type safety, enhanced tooling, and scalability.

In this chapter, we will explore the essential concepts of variables, types, and interfaces in TypeScript, focusing on how they can be applied in the development of smart contracts.

1. Variables in TypeScript

Variables in TypeScript can hold values of various types and represent data used in the execution of smart contracts. You can define variables using the `let`, `const`, and `var` keywords. However, `let` and `const` are more commonly used due to their block-scoping and immutability features.

1.1 Declaring Variables

```typescript
let contractOwner: string = "0xabcdef1234567890"; const transactionFee: number = 0.01; // in ETH
```

1.2 Variable Types

TypeScript supports a variety of variable types, including:

Primitive Types: `string`, `number`, `boolean`, `null`, `undefined`, and `bigint`.

Complex Types: `object`, `array`, and `tuple`.

Custom Types: Defined using type aliases or

interfaces. ### 1.3 Example of Variable Usage in Smart Contracts

```typescript
class SimpleStorage { private data: number;

constructor() {

this.data = 0; // initial value

}

public store(value: number): void { this.data = value;

}

public retrieve(): number { return this.data;

}

}
```

In the `SimpleStorage` example, we demonstrate how to declare a variable `data` that holds a numeric value representing stored data.

2. Types in TypeScript

TypeScript's strong typing system allows developers to define the kind of data a variable can hold. This helps catch potential errors during development, making smart contracts more robust and easier to maintain.

2.1 Built-in Types

String: Represents textual data.

Number: Represents both integers and floating-point numbers.

Boolean: Represents true/false values.

BigInt: For arbitrarily large integers, useful for financial calculations in blockchain. ### 2.2 Custom Types

You can create custom types using interfaces, type aliases, and enumerations. #### 2.2.1 Type Aliases

Type aliases allow you to create a new name for a type, making code more readable.

```typescript
type Address = string;

let sender: Address = "0xabcdef1234567890";
```

2.2.2 Enumerations

Using enums can help manage a set of related constants effectively.

```typescript
enum TransactionStatus { Pending,

Completed, Failed,

}

let      currentStatus:      TransactionStatus      =
TransactionStatus.Pending;
```

2.3 Example of Using Types in Smart Contracts

```typescript
interface IUser {

id: number; address: Address; balance: number;
```

```
}
class UserProfile implements IUser { id: number;

address: Address;

balance: number;

constructor(id: number, address: Address, balance:
number) { this.id = id;

this.address = address; this.balance = balance;

}
}
```

By using interfaces, we can define a structure for user profiles within a blockchain application, ensuring consistency and type safety.

3. Interfaces in TypeScript

Interfaces are a powerful feature of TypeScript that allow developers to define contracts for objects. This is particularly useful in smart contract development, where complex data structures may need to adhere to specific shapes.

3.1 Defining Interfaces

An interface defines the properties and methods that an object must implement.

```typescript
interface ITransaction { sender: Address; recipient:
Address; amount: number; timestamp: Date;

}
```

31

```
```

3.2 Implementing Interfaces

Classes in TypeScript can implement interfaces, ensuring they conform to the defined structure.

```typescript
class Transaction implements ITransaction { sender: Address;

recipient: Address; amount: number; timestamp: Date;

constructor(sender: Address, recipient: Address, amount: number) { this.sender = sender;

this.recipient = recipient; this.amount = amount; this.timestamp = new Date();

}

public logTransaction(): void {

console.log(`Transaction from ${this.sender} to ${this.recipient} of amount ${this.amount} at

${this.timestamp}`);

}

}
```

3.3 Extending Interfaces

TypeScript allows you to extend interfaces, which is beneficial for inheritance and ensuring code reusability.

```typescript
interface IAdvancedTransaction extends ITransaction {
```

```
transactionId: string;

isConfirmed: boolean;

}

class          AdvancedTransaction          implements
IAdvancedTransaction { sender: Address;

recipient: Address; amount: number; timestamp: Date;
transactionId: string; isConfirmed: boolean;

constructor(sender: Address, recipient: Address, amount:
number, transactionId: string) { this.sender = sender;

this.recipient  =  recipient;  this.amount  =  amount;
this.timestamp  =  new  Date();  this.transactionId  =
transactionId; this.isConfirmed = false;

}

}

```
Understanding these concepts is vital for any developer
looking to deploy effective and secure smart contracts on
the blockchain. As we progress through this book, we will
build on these foundational skills to develop complex
blockchain applications that utilize the full potential of
TypeScript.

Functions, Classes, and Modules in Blockchain Applications

TypeScript, a superset of JavaScript, has gained
popularity due to its strong typing, modern features, and
compatibility with existing JavaScript libraries. This

chapter will explore how to effectively utilize functions, classes, and modules in TypeScript for blockchain applications, enabling developers to build scalable and maintainable solutions.

Section 1: Understanding Functions in TypeScript

Functions are the building blocks of any programming language, and in TypeScript, they come with the added benefit of static typing. This can significantly reduce runtime errors, which is crucial in the high-stakes world of blockchain development where errors can lead to financial losses.

1.1 Defining Functions

In TypeScript, we can define functions using the `function` keyword, and we can specify parameter types and return types. For example:

```typescript
function calculateTransactionFee(amount: number, feePercentage: number): number { return amount * (feePercentage / 100);

}
```

1.2 Higher-Order Functions

Higher-order functions can take other functions as arguments or return them as results. This capability allows for flexible and reusable code. A common use case in blockchain applications is to handle various types of transactions:

```typescript
```

```typescript
function processTransaction(transaction: {amount:
number, feePercentage: number}, feeCalculator: (amount:
number, feePercentage: number) => number): number {

return feeCalculator(transaction.amount,
transaction.feePercentage);

}
// Example usage

const transaction = { amount: 1000, feePercentage: 2 };

const fee = processTransaction(transaction,
calculateTransactionFee); console.log(`Transaction Fee:
$${fee}`);
```
```

## Section 2: Object-Oriented Programming with Classes

TypeScript supports object-oriented programming paradigms, making it easy to model real-world entities like users, transactions, and wallets with classes. This encapsulation leads to more organized and modular code.

### 2.1 Defining Classes

Classes in TypeScript can have properties and methods, and we can leverage access modifiers to control visibility. For instance, we could create a class to represent a blockchain wallet:

```typescript
class Wallet {

private balance: number;

constructor(initialBalance: number) { this.balance =
initialBalance;
```
```

```typescript
}

public deposit(amount: number): void { this.balance +=
amount;

}

public withdraw(amount: number): boolean { if (amount >
this.balance) {

console.log('Insufficient funds'); return false;

}

this.balance -= amount; return true;

}

public getBalance(): number { return this.balance;

}

}
```

2.2 Inheritance and Polymorphism

TypeScript also supports inheritance, allowing us to derive
new classes from existing ones. For example, we could
create a specialized wallet class for cryptocurrency:

```typescript
class CryptoWallet extends Wallet { private
transactionHistory: string[] = [];

public transact(amount: number, type: 'deposit' |
'withdraw'): void { if (type === 'deposit') {

this.deposit(amount);
this.transactionHistory.push(`Deposited: $${amount}`);
```

```
    } else {
        if              (this.withdraw(amount))              {
        this.transactionHistory.push(`Withdrew: $${amount}`);
        }
    }
}

public      getHistory():      string[]      {      return
this.transactionHistory;
}
}
```

```

## Section 3: Modules for Code Organization

As blockchain applications scale, it's essential to maintain organized code through modules. TypeScript provides a robust module system that allows developers to encapsulate their code into separate files, enhancing maintainability and readability.

### 3.1 Using Modules

Modules can be created by exporting classes, functions, or variables from one file and importing them into another. For example, we could structure our code as follows:

**wallet.ts**

```typescript
export class Wallet {
// ... (implementation as above)
```
```

```
}
```

cryptoWallet.ts

```typescript
import { Wallet } from './wallet';
export class CryptoWallet extends Wallet {
// ... (implementation as above)
}
```

3.2 Organizing Blockchain Components

It's crucial to organize your application based on functionality. For example, you might create separate modules for transactions, user management, and smart contracts. This modular approach helps teams collaborate more effectively and focus on different parts of the application:

```
/src
/modules
/wallet.ts
/transaction.ts
/user.ts
/smartContract.ts
```

Each module can be developed and tested in isolation,

reducing complexity and improving the quality of the codebase.

By leveraging TypeScript's strong typing and object-oriented features, developers can create more maintainable and scalable code. As blockchain technology continues to evolve, employing these practices will be essential in building robust applications that can adapt to the changing landscape.

Chapter 3: Advanced TypeScript Concepts for Web3

While basic TypeScript features provide a solid foundation, advanced features are crucial for tackling the unique challenges posed by Web3. This chapter delves into several advanced TypeScript concepts, including generics, conditional types, and decorators, emphasizing their practical applications in the Web3 ecosystem.

3.1 Understanding Generics in TypeScript

Generics provide a way to create reusable and flexible components that can work with any data type while preserving the information about those types. In a Web3 context, generics can be particularly beneficial when dealing with smart contract interactions, where the return type can vary based on the contract's specific implementation.

3.1.1 Generic Interfaces and Functions

Consider a scenario where we want to create a utility function to interact with different token contracts. Using generics allows us to define a flexible interface that can adapt to various token standards, such as ERC20 or ERC721.

```typescript
interface Token<T> {

transfer(to: string, amount: T): Promise<boolean>;
balanceOf(account: string): Promise<T>;

}

function getTokenBalance<T>(token: Token<T>, account:
```

40

```typescript
string): Promise<T> { return token.balanceOf(account);
}
```
```

In this example, the `Token` interface is generic, allowing it to handle different types (`string`, `number`, or even `BigNumber`) depending on the token standard. By defining our functions generically, we improve code reusability and type safety.

## 3.2 Conditional Types for Dynamic Contract Interactions

Conditional types in TypeScript allow developers to define types based on conditions, enabling dynamic type resolutions. This feature is particularly useful when fetching data from various contracts, whether they are fungible or non-fungible tokens.

### 3.2.1 Using Conditional Types

Let's define a generic function that retrieves the type of a contract's return value based on the token type.

```typescript
type TokenType = 'erc20' | 'erc721';

type TokenReturnType<T extends TokenType> = T extends 'erc20'

? number // ERC20 returns numbers

: T extends 'erc721'

? string // ERC721 returns string representing a token id
```
```

```
: never;

async     function     fetchTokenData<T     extends
TokenType>(tokenType:                              T):
Promise<TokenReturnType<T>>  {  if  (tokenType  ===
'erc20') {
```

// Call the appropriate function to fetch ERC20 data
return await fetchERC20Data() as TokenReturnType<T>;

} else if (tokenType === 'erc721') {

// Call the appropriate function to fetch ERC721 data
return await fetchERC721Data() as TokenReturnType<T>;

}

throw new Error('Unsupported token type');

}

``` ` ` ` ```

In this code snippet, `TokenReturnType` specifies the
return type based on the `tokenType` provided. This
ensures that developers working with different token
standards receive the correct type, enhancing type safety.

3.3 Decorators for Smart Contract Annotations

Decorators are an advanced feature in TypeScript that
allow developers to attach metadata to classes, methods,
or properties. In the realm of Web3, decorators can be
used to enhance smart contract interactions or manage
state management effectively.

3.3.1 Creating a Simple Contract Decorator

Let's implement a simple logging decorator that
automatically logs when a method on a smart contract is
```

called:

```typescript
function LogMethodCalls(target: any, propertyKey: string, descriptor: PropertyDescriptor) { const originalMethod = descriptor.value;

descriptor.value = function (...args: any[]) { console.log(`Calling ${propertyKey} with`, args); return originalMethod.apply(this, args);
};

return descriptor;
}

class TokenContract { @LogMethodCalls

async transfer(to: string, amount: number): Promise<boolean> {

// Transfer logic

return true; // Placeholder for actual implementation

}

}
```

Here, the `LogMethodCalls` decorator wraps the `transfer` method, logging its invocation along with the arguments. This pattern enhances debugging capabilities and provides insights into contract interactions, which is crucial in the often unpredictable environment of Web3.

3.4 Utility Types for Improved Type Management

TypeScript offers several utility types that can simplify

complex type manipulations. For example, `Partial`,

`Pick`, and `Omit` can be utilized to shape existing types to fit specific use cases in smart contract development.

3.4.1 Utilizing Utility Types

Imagine we have a complex type representing a user's wallet transaction. We might want to create a new type that omits certain properties for a public view.

```typescript
interface Transaction { id: string;

amount: number; from: string;

to: string; timestamp: Date;

}

type PublicTransaction = Omit<Transaction, 'from' | 'to'>;
// Omit sensitive data const transaction:
PublicTransaction = {

id: 'tx1', amount: 100,

timestamp: new Date(),

};
```

By creating a `PublicTransaction` type using `Omit`, we ensure sensitive information is not exposed in public-facing components, adhering to privacy best practices.

Understanding and utilizing advanced TypeScript concepts is foundational for building robust and type-safe Web3 applications. Generics allow for versatile component design, conditional types facilitate dynamic

44

interactions with blockchain contracts, decorators provide a means to enhance functionality without modifying core logic, and utility types improve type management and readability.

Generics, Decorators, and Advanced Types

TypeScript, as a superset of JavaScript, brings static typing and advanced programming features that greatly enhance the development experience, especially in complex scenarios common in blockchain applications. In this chapter, we will explore generics, decorators, and advanced types in TypeScript and how they can be effectively utilized in blockchain development.

1. Understanding Generics

Generics in TypeScript provide a way to create reusable components that can work over a variety of types instead of a single one. This flexibility is especially useful in blockchain applications where data structures and types can vary widely depending on the context.

1.1 Using Generics in Smart Contracts

Consider a scenario where you need to define a data structure to handle transactions for different types of cryptocurrencies. Using generics allows you to define a function that can work with any currency type without sacrificing type safety.

```typescript
interface Transaction<T> { sender: string;
```

```
  receiver: string; amount: T;
}
function createTransaction<T>(sender: string, receiver:
string, amount: T): Transaction<T> { return { sender,
receiver, amount };
}
// Example usage:
const              ethTransaction              =
createTransaction<string>("0x123", "0x456", "1.5 ETH");
const              btcTransaction              =
createTransaction<number>("1A1zP1eP5QGefi2DMPTfTL
5SLmv7DivfNa",
"1BvBMSEYstWetqTFn5Au4m4gfMxKzM4fXi", 0.1);
```
```

In this example, `Transaction` is a generic interface that
can handle different types of `amount`, allowing for
flexible transaction handling across various
cryptocurrencies.

## 2. Decorators in TypeScript

Decorators in TypeScript offer a way to attach metadata or
modify the behavior of classes and their members at
runtime. This is particularly relevant in blockchain where
smart contracts can benefit from annotation, logging, or
validation.

### 2.1 Creating Custom Decorators

To illustrate this, let's create a simple logging decorator
that tracks the execution of smart contract methods.
```

```typescript
function LogMethod(target: any, propertyName: string, descriptor: PropertyDescriptor) { const originalMethod = descriptor.value;

descriptor.value = function (...args: any[]) {

console.log(`Calling ${propertyName} with arguments: ${JSON.stringify(args)}`);        const        result        = originalMethod.apply(this, args);

console.log(`Result: ${JSON.stringify(result)}`); return result;

};

}

class SmartContract { @LogMethod

transfer(sender: string, receiver: string, amount: number) {

// Transfer logic here

return { success: true, sender, receiver, amount };

}

}

// Example usage

const        contract        =        new        SmartContract();
contract.transfer("0x123", "0x456", 5);
```

In this example, the `LogMethod` decorator logs the method name along with its arguments and the result. This can be invaluable in smart contracts where understanding the flow of operations is crucial for debugging and auditing.

3. Advanced Types

TypeScript's powerful type system allows for sophisticated type definitions that can handle complex scenarios typical of blockchain applications.

3.1 Union and Intersection Types

Union types allow a variable to hold values of multiple types, while intersection types enable combining multiple types into one. Both can be highly beneficial in scenarios where blockchain entities can vary dramatically.

Union Types Example

```typescript
type TransactionResult = { success: true; transactionId: string } | { success: false; error: string };

function processTransaction(): TransactionResult {

// Simulate a transaction processing const success = Math.random() > 0.5;


if (success) {

return { success: true, transactionId: 'tx12345' };

} else {

return { success: false, error: 'Insufficient funds' };

}

}
```

Here, `TransactionResult` can represent either a successful transaction or an error, providing clear and type- safe handling of expected outcomes.

Intersection Types Example

```typescript
typescript interface Account {
id: string; balance: number;
}
interface Freezable { frozen: boolean;
}
type FrozenAccount = Account & Freezable; const account: FrozenAccount = {
id: '0x123',
balance: 100, frozen: false,
};
```

In this example, `FrozenAccount` combines properties of both `Account` and `Freezable`, allowing for types that reflect real-world constraints of blockchain assets.

Generics, decorators, and advanced types in TypeScript provide a powerful toolset for blockchain developers. By leveraging these features, developers can create type-safe, reusable, and maintainable code that is crucial for the dynamic and often complex landscape of blockchain technology. As the ecosystem continues to evolve, mastering these TypeScript features will empower developers to build more robust and scalable blockchain applications.

Error Handling and Debugging in Blockchain Projects

This chapter focuses on error handling and debugging techniques specifically tailored for blockchain projects using TypeScript. With TypeScript's static typing and powerful tooling, developers can build more robust applications, but leveraging these features effectively is key to achieving reliability.

Understanding Common Errors in Blockchain Applications

Before diving into error handling strategies, it's vital to understand the types of errors that commonly occur in blockchain projects:

Smart Contract Bugs: Mistakes in the logic of smart contracts can lead to unexpected behavior. For example, a common issue is integer overflow, where calculations exceed the maximum limit of the data type.

Network Errors: Blockchain operates across a distributed network, which can lead to latency issues, connection timeouts, and other network-related errors when interacting with nodes.

Transaction Failures: Transactions can fail due to various reasons, such as insufficient gas, invalid parameters, or reversion in smart contract execution. Understanding how to handle these failures gracefully is crucial.

Data Validation Errors: Input validation is critical for preventing malicious transactions or unexpected behavior in applications. Failing to validate user input can lead to errors down the line.

User Errors: Mistakes by users, such as sending ether to an incorrect address or failing to sign transactions correctly, can lead to frustration and mistrust.

Error Handling Strategies ### 1. Using Try-Catch Blocks

In TypeScript, you can leverage `try-catch` blocks to handle exceptions that may occur during execution. This is particularly important when dealing with asynchronous operations like smart contract calls or network requests.

```typescript
async function executeTransaction(tx: Transaction) { try {

const receipt = await sendTransaction(tx);
console.log('Transaction successful:', receipt);

} catch (error) {

console.error('Transaction failed:', error);

// Further error handling logic...

}

}
```

In this example, if `sendTransaction` throws an error (perhaps due to a network issue or a revert), it will be caught, allowing you to handle the situation gracefully instead of crashing the application.

2. Leveraging TypeScript's Type System

TypeScript's type system enables developers to define the possible errors more explicitly. For instance, you can create custom error classes to represent specific blockchain-related errors.

```typescript
class InsufficientGasError extends Error {
constructor(message: string) {
super(message);
this.name = 'InsufficientGasError';
}
}

function checkGasLimit(gasLimit: number) { if (gasLimit < MIN_GAS_LIMIT) {
throw new InsufficientGasError('Gas limit is too low for this transaction.');
}
}
```

By throwing specialized errors, you can handle different situations more clearly and provide more informative error messages to users and developers.

3. Using Logging Libraries

Effective logging is essential for diagnosing issues in production. Using a structured logging library can help you capture detailed information about errors and system behavior. Libraries like `winston` or `bunyan` can be integrated easily into TypeScript projects.

```typescript
import { createLogger, transports, format } from 'winston';

const logger = createLogger({ level: 'info',

format:               format.combine(format.timestamp(),
format.json()), transports: [

new transports.Console(),

new transports.File({ filename: 'error.log', level: 'error' }),

],

});

logger.error('Transaction failed', { error });
```

By logging structured information about the errors, developers and support teams can identify patterns and replicate issues more efficiently, making debugging easier.

Debugging Techniques

1. Using TypeScript with Development Tools

TypeScript's integration with development tools like Visual Studio Code provides powerful debugging functionalities. You can set breakpoints, inspect variables, and step through your code to identify issues in real time.

2. Smart Contract Testing Frameworks

Before deploying smart contracts, using frameworks like Hardhat or Truffle allows you to simulate transactions and test your contracts against various scenarios. This can help catch logic errors early on.

```typescript
import { expect } from 'chai'; import { ethers } from 'hardhat';

describe('MySmartContract', function () {

it('should revert if gas limit is insufficient', async function () { const contract = await MySmartContract.deploy();

await expect(contract.someFunction({ gasLimit: 100 })).to.be.revertedWith('Insufficient gas');

});

});
```

3. Analysing Transaction Logs

Blockchain transactions are immutable but traceable. By examining transaction logs or events, you can identify where things went wrong. In Ethereum, for example, `web3.js` or `ethers.js` provides tooling to easily access these logs.

4. Using Monitoring Tools

In live environments, integrating monitoring tools can help track the performance of your application and its interactions with the blockchain network. Solutions like Chainlink or Fortify can provide alerts on certain conditions or errors, enabling proactive fixes.

Best Practices

Always validate inputs: Ensuring the correctness of

user-supplied data can prevent many errors from cropping up after the fact.

Document error codes: When developing APIs or smart contracts, documenting the errors users might encounter can improve the developer experience.

Implement graceful degradation: Ensure that your app continues to function, even if specific parts fail. For instance, if a transaction fails, allow the user to adjust parameters rather than locking them out.

Stay updated with security practices: Regularly audit your smart contracts using tools like MythX or Slither to catch potential vulnerabilities.

By leveraging TypeScript's capabilities alongside best practices in error handling, developers can build more reliable applications. Ultimately, a proactive approach to error handling can reduce downtime, enhance user experience, and build trust in blockchain technology's promise of security and transparency.

Chapter 4: Introduction to Blockchain and Smart Contracts

Unlike traditional databases, where a single entity controls the information, blockchain operates on a distributed network, meaning that every participant has access to an identical copy of the ledger. This decentralization not only enhances security but also builds trust among its users.

4.1.1 The Structure of a Blockchain

A blockchain consists of a series of blocks, each containing a list of transactions and a unique cryptographic hash of the previous block. This structure ensures that any alteration in the data of one block would require changes to all subsequent blocks, making the tampering nearly impossible. Each block also contains a timestamp, which adds a time dimension to the data stored. Together, these features create an immutable record of transactions, where the integrity and authenticity of the information are preserved.

4.1.2 Key Characteristics of Blockchain

The distinguishing features of blockchain include:

Decentralization: Eliminates the need for intermediaries, such as banks or brokers, allowing peer-to- peer transactions.

Transparency: All transactions are recorded on the public ledger, visible to all participants in the network, fostering trust and accountability.

Security: Advanced cryptographic techniques protect the data, making it resistant to hacking and fraud.

Immutability: Once a block is added to the chain, it cannot be altered or deleted, providing a permanent record of transactions.

These characteristics make blockchain an attractive solution for a wide range of applications, from finance and supply chain management to healthcare and voting systems.

4.2 The Emergence of Smart Contracts

Building on the foundation laid by blockchain technology, smart contracts represent a significant leap in how agreements are executed and enforced. Coined by cryptographer Nick Szabo in the 1990s, smart contracts are self-executing contracts with the terms of the agreement directly written into code. These digital contracts run on the blockchain, allowing them to be executed automatically once predetermined conditions are met.

4.2.1 How Smart Contracts Work

Smart contracts operate through a series of 'if-then' statements, enabling conditional logic. For instance, a simple smart contract for an online purchase might stipulate that if payment is received (the condition), then the product will be automatically delivered (the result). This automatic execution eliminates the need for intermediaries, significantly reducing transaction times and costs.

The execution of smart contracts is also governed by the consensus mechanism used by the blockchain network. For example, in a Proof of Work (PoW) system, miners validate transactions by solving complex mathematical puzzles, while in Proof of Stake (PoS), validators are selected based on the number of coins they hold and are willing to "stake." Once consensus is reached, the smart contract is executed, ensuring that all parties adhere to the agreed-upon terms. ### 4.2.2 Benefits of Smart Contracts

The advantages of smart contracts include:

Efficiency: Automated execution reduces the time required to complete transactions.

Cost-effectiveness: By removing intermediaries, smart contracts lower transaction fees.

Trust: The self-executing nature of smart contracts fosters trust among parties, as there's no risk of manipulation or breach.

Accuracy: Smart contracts are executed exactly as programmed, minimizing the risk of error associated with manual contract management.

These benefits are causing industries worldwide to explore the potential of smart contracts in transforming their operations.

4.3 Applications of Blockchain and Smart Contracts

The versatility of blockchain and smart contracts has led to numerous applications across various sectors:

Finance and Banking: Blockchain facilitates secure transactions with reduced fees and faster settlement times. Smart contracts automate processes like loan approvals and insurance claims, improving efficiency in the financial sector.

Supply Chain Management: Companies can utilize blockchain to trace the origin of products, ensuring transparency and accountability in the supply chain. Smart contracts can automate payments and inventory management based on real-time data.

Healthcare: Blockchain can enhance patient data management and interoperability among healthcare providers. Smart contracts can automate reimbursements from insurance companies based on the delivery of medical services.

Voting Systems: Blockchain technology offers a secure and transparent method for conducting elections. Smart contracts can ensure that votes are validated and counted in a tamper-proof manner.

4.4 Challenges and Future Outlook

Despite the immense potential of blockchain and smart contracts, several challenges remain. Issues such as scalability, energy consumption, regulatory compliance, and the need for standardization must be addressed to unlock the full capabilities of these technologies. Furthermore, as with any emerging technology, public understanding and acceptance are critical for widespread adoption.

As the world continues to embrace digital transformation, the future of blockchain and smart contracts looks promising. With ongoing advancements in technology and a growing ecosystem of developers, businesses, and policymakers committed to fostering innovation, we can anticipate a transformative impact on how we transact, contract, and interact in the digital age.

How Blockchain Works: Key Concepts & Architecture

Originally created as the underlying technology for Bitcoin, blockchain has evolved into a platform that enables secure, transparent, and decentralized applications across various industries. In this chapter, we will explore the fundamental concepts of blockchain, its architecture, and how it operates to reshape the landscape of digital transactions.

What is Blockchain?

At its core, a blockchain is a distributed ledger technology that allows multiple parties to maintain a shared, immutable record of transactions. This decentralized system eliminates the need for a central authority, making processes more efficient and reducing the risk of fraud. Each block in the chain contains a list of transactions, and once recorded, these transactions cannot be altered without consensus from the network participants.

Key Characteristics of Blockchain

Before diving deeper into how blockchain works, it is essential to acknowledge its key characteristics:

Decentralization: Unlike traditional databases that are controlled by a central entity, blockchain operates on a peer-to-peer network. This decentralization means that every participant (or node) in the network has access to the entire ledger, promoting transparency and reducing the risk of single points of failure.

Immutability: Once data is added to the blockchain, it

becomes nearly impossible to alter. This is ensured through cryptographic techniques that secure the data, making it tamper-proof and providing an auditable history of transactions.

Transparency: All transactions on a blockchain are visible to all participants. This level of transparency fosters trust among users, as anyone can verify the transactions without needing to rely on a central authority.

Consensus Mechanisms: To validate transactions and add new blocks to the chain, participants must agree on the order and validity of transactions. This is achieved through consensus mechanisms, such as Proof of Work (PoW), Proof of Stake (PoS), and others.

Key Components of Blockchain

Understanding blockchain requires familiarity with its essential components: ### 1. Blocks

A block is the fundamental unit of a blockchain. Each block contains three primary elements:

Data: This includes transaction details, timestamps, and any other pertinent information.

Nonce: A random number used to create a hash. The nonce is crucial for the mining process in PoW blockchains.

Hash: A unique identifier for the block. The hash is generated from the block's data, ensuring that even the slightest modification will result in a completely different hash.

2. Chain

The "chain" connects blocks in a sequential manner. Each block references the hash of the previous block, creating an unbreakable link. This structure ensures that any changes to one block will necessitate changes to all subsequent blocks, making tampering evident.

3. Nodes

Nodes are individual participants in the blockchain network. They maintain copies of the entire blockchain and work together to update the ledger. Depending on their role, nodes can be classified as:

Full Nodes: These nodes maintain a complete copy of the blockchain and verify transactions independently.

Light Nodes: These nodes store only a portion of the blockchain and rely on full nodes for validation. ### 4. Consensus Mechanisms

Consensus mechanisms are protocols that ensure all nodes in the network agree on the validity of transactions before they are added to the blockchain. Common consensus mechanisms include:

Proof of Work (PoW): Miners solve complex mathematical problems to validate transactions. This process is energy-intensive and serves as a deterrent against malicious activity.

Proof of Stake (PoS): Validators are chosen based on the number of coins they hold and are willing to "stake." This method is more energy-efficient than PoW.

Delegated Proof of Stake (DPoS): A variation where stakeholders elect delegates who validate transactions on their behalf.

How Blockchain Works: The Process

The operation of blockchain can be summarized in several key steps:

Step 1: Transaction Initiation

A user initiates a transaction, which is then broadcasted to the network. Each transaction contains details such as the sender's and receiver's addresses and the amount being transferred.

Step 2: Validation

Transactions must be verified by the network through consensus mechanisms. For example, in a PoW system, miners will compete to solve cryptographic puzzles. The first one to succeed gets to add the block of transactions to the blockchain.

Step 3: Block Creation

Once validated, the transactions are bundled into a block. This block is then created with its unique hash, hash of the previous block, and nonce.

Step 4: Addition to the Chain

The newly created block is added to the existing blockchain, and all nodes in the network are updated. This stage marks the completion of the transaction.

Step 5: Confirmation

Once the block is added, the transactions within it are considered confirmed. The block will eventually receive multiple confirmations as subsequent blocks are added, increasing the security of the recorded transactions.

By eliminating the need for intermediaries and providing a tamper-proof record, blockchain is revolutionizing trust in the digital age. As the technology continues to evolve, understanding its core concepts and architecture will be paramount for businesses and individuals looking to harness its potential. In subsequent chapters, we will delve into real-world applications of blockchain and explore its implications across various sectors.

Smart Contracts: What They Are & How They Function

Unlike traditional contracts that require intermediaries to enforce their terms, smart contracts run on blockchain technology, which ensures transparency, security, and immutability. They can facilitate, verify, or enforce the negotiation or performance of a contract.

The Ethereum blockchain is the most well-known platform for developing smart contracts, although other blockchains like Binance Smart Chain, Polkadot, and Solana also support their functionality. Smart contracts enable decentralized applications (dApps) by allowing complex logic to be executed on-chain, thus making them integral to the Web3 ecosystem.

Core Features of Smart Contracts

Self-Execution: Once placed on the blockchain, smart contracts automatically enforce and execute the agreed terms without human intervention.

Transparency: All contract terms are visible and unchangeable on the blockchain, ensuring parties can verify the contract at any time.

Security: The cryptographic nature of blockchain technology protects against tampering, making smart contracts secure and reliable.

Cost-Efficiency: By eliminating intermediaries, smart contracts reduce transaction costs and delays.

Accuracy: Due to the automated nature of smart contracts, they minimize human errors typically associated with traditional contract handling.

How Smart Contracts Function

Basic Components of a Smart Contract

To understand how smart contracts work, it's essential to break down their components:

Code: This defines the rules and logic of the smart contract. It is often written in languages such as Solidity for Ethereum but can also be written in TypeScript for frameworks like TypeChain.

State: This refers to the condition or status of the contract at any given time. The state is stored on the blockchain.

Events: Smart contracts can emit events to inform users when a particular action has occurred, enabling easy tracking of contract interactions.

Functions: These are the operations that can be performed on the smart contract, such as reading or modifying the state.

The Lifecycle of a Smart Contract

Development: Developers write the smart contract code, typically using a language like Solidity or TypeScript.

Deployment: The compiled contract is deployed onto a blockchain network where it is assigned a unique address.

Interaction: Users can interact with the contract via transactions, calling functions to read from or modify the contract state.

Execution: The smart contract's code executes automatically based on its logic whenever the specified conditions are met.

Event Emission: Upon execution, the contract may emit events, which can be monitored by external applications or interfaces.

Writing Smart Contracts in TypeScript

While TypeScript is not a primary language for deploying smart contracts directly on blockchains, it can be utilized in conjunction with frameworks like TypeChain. These frameworks can generate TypeScript typings for contract interactions, enabling a more seamless development experience within TypeScript-based applications.

Setting Up the Development Environment

To get started with smart contracts in TypeScript, follow these steps:

Install Node.js: Ensure you have Node.js installed on your machine.

Initialize a New Project:

```bash
mkdir my-smart-contract cd my-smart-contract npm init -y
```

```
```

Install Dependencies:

```bash
npm install --save-dev typescript ts-node typechain @nomiclabs/hardhat ethers
```

Setup TypeChain: Create a Hardhat project and configure it for TypeChain to generate types for contract interactions.

Writing a Sample Smart Contract

Let's create a simple storage smart contract to demonstrate how you would structure it in Solidity, and then use TypeScript for interacting with it.

Smart Contract in Solidity (Storage.sol):

```solidity
// SPDX-License-Identifier: MIT pragma solidity ^0.8.0;

contract Storage { uint256 private value;

event ValueChanged(uint256 newValue); function setValue(uint256 newValue) public {

value = newValue;

emit ValueChanged(newValue);

}

function getValue() public view returns (uint256) { return value;

}
```

```
}
```
```

**TypeScript Interaction (index.ts)**:

```typescript
import { ethers } from "hardhat";

import { Storage__factory } from "../typechain";

async function main() {

// Deploy the contract

const storageFactory = new Storage__factory();

const storageContract = await storageFactory.deploy();
await storageContract.deployed();

console.log("Storage contract deployed to:", storageContract.address);


// Set a value

const tx = await storageContract.setValue(42); await tx.wait();


// Get the value

const currentValue = await storageContract.getValue();
console.log("Current value in storage:", currentValue.toString());
}
// Execute the script main().catch((error) => {
```
```

```
console.error(error); process.exitCode = 1;
});
```
` ` `

Explanation of the TypeScript Code In the above TypeScript code:

Importing Modules: We import necessary modules from the Hardhat framework to facilitate contract deployment and interaction.

Deploying the Contract: Using a factory pattern, we deploy our `Storage` contract to the blockchain.

Setting and Getting Values: We call the `setValue` function to change the stored value, then retrieve it using `getValue`.

By leveraging blockchain's immutable nature and employing programming languages like TypeScript for interactions, developers can create robust decentralized applications. Understanding the intricate dynamics of smart contracts is essential for anyone looking to innovate in the blockchain space.

Chapter 5: Setting Up a TypeScript-Based Blockchain Development Environment

This chapter will guide you through the essential tools, libraries, and configurations to start building your decentralized applications (dApps) using TypeScript.

5.1 Introduction to TypeScript in Blockchain Development

TypeScript is a superset of JavaScript that adds static typing to the language, making it more robust and easier to maintain. Its use in blockchain development is growing due to the following advantages:

Type Safety: Helps catch errors at compile time rather than runtime.

Improved Tooling: Offers better autocompletion and navigation features in IDEs.

Object-Oriented Programming: Supports modern programming paradigms, making complex applications easier to manage.

With these advantages in mind, let's proceed with setting up our environment. ### 5.2 Prerequisites

Before diving into the setup, ensure you have the following prerequisites:

Node.js and npm: We'll be using Node.js as our runtime environment. npm (Node Package Manager) will help us manage our project dependencies. You can download them from nodejs.org.

TypeScript: This is the core of our development, so

make sure to install TypeScript globally:

```bash
npm install -g typescript
```

Git: Essential for version control and collaboration. Install Git from git-scm.com.

A code editor: While you can use any code editor, Visual Studio Code (VSCode) is highly recommended due to its excellent TypeScript support and debugging capabilities.

5.3 Setting Up Your Project #### 5.3.1 Create a New Directory

Let's create a new directory for your blockchain project:

```bash
mkdir my-blockchain-dapp cd my-blockchain-dapp
```

5.3.2 Initialize npm

Now, initialize a new npm project. This will create a `package.json` file where we can manage our project dependencies.

```bash npm init -y
```

5.3.3 Install TypeScript Locally

Though we installed TypeScript globally, we should also install it as a local dependency:

```bash
```

```
npm install typescript --save-dev
```

5.3.4 Create a TypeScript Configuration File

Next, create a `tsconfig.json` file to configure the TypeScript compiler options. You can easily create this file using the following command:

```bash
npx tsc --init
```

This will generate a basic `tsconfig.json` file. You may want to modify it according to your project needs. A common configuration might look like this:

```json
{
"compilerOptions": { "target": "es6", "module": "commonjs", "strict": true, "esModuleInterop": true, "skipLibCheck": true,

"forceConsistentCasingInFileNames": true, "outDir": "./dist"
},
"include": ["./src/**/*"],

"exclude": ["node_modules", "**/*.spec.ts"]

}
```

5.4 Installing Blockchain Libraries

To build blockchain applications, we'll need additional libraries. The choice of libraries often depends on the blockchain you wish to work with. For the purpose of this chapter, let's consider Ethereum and the popular libraries used in its ecosystem.

5.4.1 Install ethers.js

`ethers.js` is a library that provides a simple and intuitive way to interact with the Ethereum blockchain:

```bash
npm install ethers
```

5.4.2 Install Hardhat

Hardhat is a development environment to compile, deploy, test, and debug your Ethereum software. Install it in your project directory:

```bash
npm install --save-dev hardhat
```

After installing, you can initialize Hardhat with the following command:

```bash
npx hardhat
```

Follow the prompts to create a basic sample project. This setup will create a `hardhat.config.ts` file where you can configure various aspects of your development environment.

5.5 Folder Structure

A well-organized project structure greatly enhances productivity and maintainability. Here's a recommended folder structure for your TypeScript-based blockchain project:

```
` ` `

my-blockchain-dapp/

contracts/     # Smart contracts MyContract.sol

scripts/       # Deployment scripts deploy.ts

test/    # Test files MyContract.test.ts

src/     # TypeScript source code index.ts
utils.ts

dist/   # Compiled output node_modules/      #     npm packages package.json
tsconfig.json

hardhat.config.ts
` ` `
```

5.6 Writing Your First Smart Contract

Now that your environment is set up, let's write a simple Ethereum smart contract. Navigate to the

`contracts` directory and create a file named `MyContract.sol`:

```solidity
// SPDX-License-Identifier: MIT pragma solidity ^0.8.0;

contract MyContract { string public message;

constructor(string memory initialMessage) { message = initialMessage;

}

function updateMessage(string memory newMessage) public { message = newMessage;

}

}
```

5.7 Compiling and Testing Your Smart Contract To compile your smart contract, run:

```bash
npx hardhat compile
```

For testing, create a new file `MyContract.test.ts` in the `test` directory and write your tests using the Mocha framework, supported by Hardhat.

We covered the installation of essential tools, libraries, and a practical approach to building your first smart contract. As you move forward, keep experimenting and expand your knowledge of TypeScript and blockchain interaction.

Installing Node.js, TypeScript, and Web3 Libraries

In this chapter, we will guide you through the essential steps to set up your development environment for building decentralized applications (dApps) using Node.js, TypeScript, and the Web3 libraries. These tools form the backbone of many blockchain projects, allowing for seamless interactions with smart contracts and blockchain networks. By the end of this chapter, you will have a fully configured environment ready for blockchain development.

1. Prerequisites

Before diving into the installations, make sure you have the following:

A computer with internet access.

Basic understanding of JavaScript and TypeScript.

Familiarity with the command line/terminal. ## 2. Installing Node.js

Node.js is a runtime environment that allows developers to run JavaScript code on the server side. It includes the Node Package Manager (npm), which we will use to install TypeScript and Web3 libraries.

Step-by-Step Installation:

Download and Install Node.js:

Visit the official Node.js website: https://nodejs.org/.

You will see two versions available: LTS (Long Term Support) and Current. It's recommended to download the LTS version for stability.

Download the installer for your operating system (Windows, macOS, or Linux) and run it.

Follow the installation instructions provided by the installer.

Verify Installation:

After installation, open your terminal (Command Prompt on Windows, Terminal on macOS/Linux) and type the following commands to verify the installation:

```bash
node -v npm -v
```

You should see the version numbers for both Node.js and npm, indicating that they were installed successfully.

3. Setting Up a Project Directory

It's time to create a new directory for your project where you will work with Node.js and TypeScript.

Create a Directory:

In your terminal, navigate to the location where you want to create your project and run:

```bash
mkdir my-dapp cd my-dapp
```

Initialize a Node.js Project:

Run the following command to create a `package.json` file, which will hold your project configurations and dependencies:

```bash
npm init -y
```

The `-y` flag automatically generates a default `package.json` file without prompting for any information. ## 4. Installing TypeScript

TypeScript is a superset of JavaScript that adds static types. This can help avoid bugs and improve the development experience.

Step-by-Step Installation:

Install TypeScript Globally:

To use TypeScript globally, you can install it via npm:

```bash
npm install -g typescript
```

This command installs the TypeScript compiler, allowing you to compile TypeScript files into JavaScript.

Verify TypeScript Installation:

To confirm that TypeScript was installed correctly, run:

```bash
tsc -v
```

You should see the version number of TypeScript.

Initialize TypeScript in your Project:

In your project directory, run the following command to create a `tsconfig.json` file, which will hold the configuration settings for your TypeScript project:

```bash
tsc --init
```

This file contains default settings, which you can modify based on your project requirements. ## 5. Installing Web3 Libraries

Web3.js is a popular library that allows you to interact with the Ethereum blockchain and its smart contracts. ### Step-by-Step Installation:

Install Web3.js:

Run the following command in your project directory to install the Web3 library:

```bash
npm install web3
```

Verify Web3 Installation:

You can check if Web3.js was installed correctly by looking at your `package.json` file or by checking the

`node_modules` directory within your project. ## 6. Setting Up Your First TypeScript File

Now that you have installed all necessary tools, you can create your first TypeScript file to interact with the

79

Ethereum blockchain.

Create an Entry File:

Inside your project directory, create a file named `index.ts`:

```bash
touch index.ts
```

Edit the File:

Open `index.ts` in your favorite code editor and add the following basic code snippet:

```typescript
import Web3 from 'web3';

const web3 = new Web3('https://mainnet.infura.io/v3/YOUR_INFURA_PROJECT_ID');
web3.eth.getBlockNumber().then(console.log);
```

Make sure to replace `YOUR_INFURA_PROJECT_ID` with your actual Infura project ID, which you can obtain by signing up at [Infura](https://infura.io/).

Compile TypeScript to JavaScript:

To compile your TypeScript code into JavaScript, run:

```bash tsc
```

This will generate an `index.js` file in the same directory.

Run Your Code:

Finally, you can execute your JavaScript file using Node.js:

```bash
node index.js
```

If everything is set up correctly, you should see the latest block number from the Ethereum blockchain printed in your terminal.

In the following chapters, we will explore more complex interactions with the Ethereum blockchain, manage smart contracts, and develop user interfaces for our dApps. This foundational chapter equips you with the essential tools and knowledge needed to delve deeper into blockchain development. Happy coding!

Configuring Hardhat, Ethers.js, and Other Essential Tools

This chapter will walk you through the process of configuring Hardhat and Ethers.js in a TypeScript environment, as well as introduce other essential tools to streamline your blockchain development experience.

Prerequisites

Before diving into the configuration, ensure you have the following installed:

Node.js: Download and install Node.js from nodejs.org. Ensure you have version 12 or higher.

npm/yarn: Node package manager (npm) is typically bundled with Node.js. Yarn can be installed separately if preferred for package management.

Setting Up Your Project

Create a New Project Directory:

Begin by creating a new directory for your blockchain project.

```bash
mkdir my-blockchain-project cd my-blockchain-project
```

Initialize a New Node.js Project:

Execute the following command to set up a `package.json` file.

```bash npm init -y
```

Install Hardhat:

Install Hardhat and TypeScript as development dependencies.

```bash
npm install --save-dev hardhat typescript ts-node @types/node
```

Create a Hardhat Project:

Next, create a new Hardhat project. When prompted,

select "Create a JavaScript project" for simplicity, as we will convert the configurations manually into TypeScript.

```bash
npx hardhat
```

This command will generate a sample project structure, including contracts, scripts, and tests.

Configuring TypeScript

Create a TypeScript Configuration File:

Create a `tsconfig.json` file to configure TypeScript settings specifically for Hardhat and your project.

```json
{
"compilerOptions": { "target": "es6", "module": "commonjs", "strict": true, "esModuleInterop": true, "skipLibCheck": true,

"forceConsistentCasingInFileNames": true
},
"include": [ "scripts", "test",
"hardhat.config.ts", "contracts/**/*"
]
}
```

Rename Hardhat Config:

Rename the `hardhat.config.js` file to `hardhat.config.ts` and adapt its content to TypeScript. Your updated configuration might look like this:

```typescript
import { task } from "hardhat/config"; import "@nomiclabs/hardhat-waffle";

const { ethers } = require("hardhat");

task("accounts", "Prints the list of accounts", async () => {
const accounts = await ethers.getSigners();

for (const account of accounts) {
console.log(account.address);
}
});
export default { solidity: "0.8.4",
};
```

This structure allows for TypeScript type-checking and better code quality. ## Integrating Ethers.js

Install Ethers.js:

Install Ethers.js, which will help you interact with the Ethereum blockchain.

```bash
npm install --save ethers
```

Using Ethers.js in Scripts:

Ethers.js can be used in your TypeScript scripts to deploy contracts and interact with the blockchain. Here's an example script showing how to deploy a simple contract:

```typescript
import { ethers } from "hardhat";

async function main() {
  const MyContract = await ethers.getContractFactory("MyContract");
  const myContract = await MyContract.deploy();

  console.log("MyContract deployed to:", myContract.address);
}

main()
.then(() => process.exit(0))
.catch((error) => { console.error(error); process.exit(1);
});
```

Essential Tools and Plugins

In addition to Hardhat and Ethers.js, consider adding the following tools and plugins to enhance your development process:

Hardhat Plugins:

Various plugins can be added to Hardhat to support specific functionalities:

@nomiclabs/hardhat-waffle: Enables testing with

Waffle.

@nomiclabs/hardhat-ethers: Provides Ethers.js support.

solidity-coverage: Allows you to measure Solidity code coverage. To add a plugin, simply use `npm install`, for example:

```bash
npm install --save-dev @nomiclabs/hardhat-ethers
```

Environment Variables:

Store sensitive data (like private keys and APIs) using the `dotenv` package for better security.

```bash
npm install --save dotenv
```

Create a `.env` file in your project root:

``` INFURA_PROJECT_ID=your_infura_project_id

PRIVATE_KEY=your_private_key
```

TypeScript Type Definitions:

Always ensure that you include type definitions for libraries you use for a smooth TypeScript experience.

```bash
npm install --save-dev @types/node
```

```
```

The potential for enhanced type-checking with TypeScript improves code quality and reduces the likelihood of runtime errors. As you build out your blockchain applications, experimenting with different Hardhat plugins and tools will further enhance your workflow and productivity.

Chapter 6: Writing Your First Smart Contract in TypeScript

In this chapter, we will take a hands-on approach to writing your first smart contract using TypeScript, a statically typed superset of JavaScript. With TypeScript's strong type checking and modern features, it provides a robust environment for developing smart contracts that are both reliable and maintainable.

6.1 Understanding Smart Contracts

Before we start coding, it's essential to grasp what a smart contract is. A smart contract is a self-executing contract with the terms of the agreement directly written into code. These contracts run on blockchain platforms (most commonly Ethereum) and have key attributes:

Autonomous: Once deployed, they operate independently, removing the need for intermediaries.

Immutable: Smart contracts cannot be modified after deployment, ensuring trust in the transaction history.

Transparent: All transactions are publicly verifiable, enhancing accountability. ## 6.2 Setting Up Your Development Environment

To write your smart contract in TypeScript, we need to set up a suitable environment. Here's a step-by-step guide:

Install Node.js: Download and install the latest version of Node.js from nodejs.org. This will bring in npm (Node Package Manager), which we will use for package management.

Create a New Directory:

```bash
mkdir MySmartContract cd MySmartContract
```

Initialize Your Project: This step creates a `package.json` file.

```bash npm init -y
```

Install TypeScript and Development Dependencies:

```bash
npm install typescript ts-node @types/node --save-dev
```

Set Up TypeScript Configuration: Create a `tsconfig.json` file in your project root with the following content:

```json
{
"compilerOptions": { "target": "ES2020", "module": "commonjs", "strict": true,

"outDir": "./dist", "esModuleInterop": true,
},
"include": ["src/**/*.ts"], "exclude": ["node_modules"]
}
```

Create Your Project Structure:

```bash
mkdir src
```

6.3 Writing Your First Smart Contract

Now that your environment is set up, let's write a simple smart contract. We'll create a simple contract for a Token that allows minting and transferring tokens.

Create a New File: Create a file named `Token.ts` in the `src` directory.

Write Your Smart Contract:

Here's a straightforward implementation of an ERC20-like token:

```typescript
// src/Token.ts class Token {

private balances: { [address: string]: number } = {};
private totalSupply: number = 0;

constructor(initialSupply:          number)          {
this.mint(initialSupply);

}

mint(amount:  number):  void  {  this.totalSupply  +=
amount;

this.balances["contractOwner"]                    =
(this.balances["contractOwner"]  ||  0)  +  amount;
console.log(`${amount} tokens  minted. Total supply is
now ${this.totalSupply}.`);

}
```

```
transfer(to: string, amount: number): boolean {

if (this.balances["contractOwner"] >= amount) {
this.balances["contractOwner"] -= amount;
this.balances[to] = (this.balances[to] || 0) + amount;
console.log(`Transferred ${amount} tokens to ${to}.`);
return true;

} else {

console.log(`Transfer failed. Insufficient balance.`);
return false;

}

}

getBalance(address: string): number { return
this.balances[address] || 0;

}

}

// Example use case

const myToken = new Token(1000);
myToken.transfer("Alice", 200);

console.log(`Alice's                                balance:
${myToken.getBalance("Alice")}`);
```
```

## 6.4 Running Your Smart Contract

To run your smart contract and see it in action, we will use `ts-node`, which allows us to execute TypeScript files directly. From your terminal, run:
```

```bash
npx ts-node src/Token.ts
```

You should see output representing the minting of tokens and the transfer to Alice, along with her balance. ## 6.5 Deploying Your Smart Contract

While this chapter has focused on writing and testing a basic smart contract in TypeScript, deploying smart contracts typically requires using specialized tools and frameworks. Here's a brief overview of the deployment process:

Choose a Blockchain: Most likely, you'll want to deploy your smart contract to a blockchain like Ethereum, Binance Smart Chain, or Polygon.

Use a Framework: Consider using frameworks like Hardhat or Truffle, which simplify the process of compiling, deploying, and testing smart contracts.

Write Deployment Scripts: Create deployment scripts in TypeScript and run them to deploy your smart contract to the blockchain.

In this chapter, we covered the basics of smart contracts, set up a development environment, created a simple token contract, and explored how to run it. As you progress, you will also want to explore more complex contracts, security best practices, and advanced features of blockchain platforms.

Introduction to Solidity with TypeScript

One of the most significant advancements in this domain is the concept of smart contracts—self-executing contracts with the terms of the agreement directly written into code.

Smart contracts run on blockchain networks, and they enable automated processes without intermediaries. Among various blockchain platforms, Ethereum is the most popular for deploying smart contracts, thanks to its robustness and flexibility. The primary programming language used to write smart contracts on Ethereum is Solidity.

1.2 What is Solidity?

Solidity is a statically typed, high-level programming language designed specifically for developing smart contracts on blockchain platforms, especially Ethereum. It was influenced by various languages, including JavaScript, C++, and Python, which makes it relatively approachable for developers familiar with those languages. Solidity provides developers with the tools needed to construct complex decentralized applications (DApps) that can interact with other smart contracts and the underlying blockchain.

With Solidity, developers can define contract structures, state variables, functions, and even event listeners, which are essential for enabling interaction with their DApps. Solid understanding of Solidity is crucial for anyone looking to build applications in the Ethereum ecosystem.

1.3 Why Use TypeScript?

TypeScript is a superset of JavaScript that introduces static typing, interfaces, and improved tooling through type definitions. These features make TypeScript an appealing choice for large-scale applications as it helps catch errors during development, improves code maintainability, and enhances developer productivity through better IDE support.

In the context of Solidity development, TypeScript can be particularly useful for several reasons:

Type Safety: Writing TypeScript enables developers to catch type-related errors at compile time rather than runtime, reducing the risk of bugs that could lead to vulnerabilities in smart contracts.

Development Experience: TypeScript provides a richer development experience through features like autocompletion, code navigation, and advanced tooling— all of which can dramatically improve developer productivity.

Integration with JavaScript Libraries: Many Ethereum-based applications require integration with JavaScript libraries. TypeScript's compatibility with these libraries makes it a seamless choice when building DApps.

Community and Ecosystem: The growth of TypeScript has resulted in a robust community and a wealth of resources, libraries, and frameworks that can simplify and enrich the development experience.

1.4 Setting Up the Development Environment

Before diving into coding, setting up a proper development environment is crucial. The following tools and frameworks are often employed when developing with Solidity and TypeScript:

Node.js: Ensure Node.js is installed on your machine.

It provides the runtime for JavaScript and TypeScript applications.

Truffle Framework: This popular development framework for Ethereum allows you to build, test, and deploy smart contracts. It also supports integration with TypeScript.

TypeScript Compiler: Install the TypeScript compiler globally using npm to transpile TypeScript code into JavaScript.

```bash
npm install -g typescript
```

Solidity Compiler (solc): The Solidity compiler is needed to compile Solidity code into bytecode that can be deployed on an Ethereum network.

Hardhat: An alternative to Truffle, Hardhat provides a development environment that allows you to compile, deploy, test, and debug Ethereum software. It has excellent TypeScript support and is favored for newer projects.

IDE or Code Editor: A modern code editor like Visual Studio Code supports TypeScript and can enhance your development workflow with extensions for Solidity, debugging, and more.

1.5 First Steps with Solidity and TypeScript

Having set up the environment, it's time to dive into your first Solidity contract using TypeScript. Below is a basic outline of creating a simple "Hello World" smart contract, migrating it, and interacting with it using TypeScript.

Step 1: Create a Simple Solidity Contract Create a file named `HelloWorld.sol`:

```solidity
// SPDX-License-Identifier: MIT pragma solidity ^0.8.0;

contract HelloWorld {

string public greetMessage;

constructor(string memory _message) { greetMessage = _message;
}

function greet() public view returns (string memory) {
return greetMessage;

}

}
```

Step 2: Compile the Contract

Use Truffle or Hardhat to compile your Solidity contract in your terminal:

```bash
truffle compile # if using Truffle
``` or

```bash
npx hardhat compile # if using Hardhat
```

Step 3: Interact with Your Contract Using TypeScript
Create an interaction script in TypeScript, `interact.ts`:

```typescript
import { ethers } from 'hardhat';

async function main() {

const HelloWorld = await ethers.getContractFactory('HelloWorld'); const helloWorld = await HelloWorld.deploy("Hello, world!");

await helloWorld.deployed();

console.log(`Contract deployed at: ${helloWorld.address}`); const message = await helloWorld.greet();

console.log(`The greeting message is: ${message}`);

}

main()

.then(() => process.exit(0))

.catch((error) => { console.error(error); process.exit(1);

});
```

Run the TypeScript script to deploy the contract and interact with it:

```bash
npx hardhat run scripts/interact.ts
```

This chapter explored the fundamentals of Solidity and

TypeScript, emphasizing their roles in creating robust decentralized applications. With the foundations laid, you are well-positioned to delve deeper into advanced topics, including contract security, gas optimization, and integration with various Ethereum-based protocols.

Writing and Deploying a Simple Smart Contract

This chapter will walk you through writing and deploying a simple smart contract using TypeScript. ## Prerequisites

Before diving into smart contract development, ensure that you have the following tools and libraries installed:

Node.js: Version 14 or higher to run JavaScript code and manage packages.

TypeScript: Install TypeScript globally via npm:

```bash
npm install -g typescript
```

Hardhat: A development environment for Ethereum that enables writing, deploying, and testing smart contracts. Install it via npm:

```bash
npm install --save-dev hardhat
```

Ethereum Wallet (e.g., MetaMask): For deploying

contracts on a test network.

Infura or Alchemy Account: To connect to an Ethereum node. ## Setting Up the Project

Create a Project Directory:

```bash
mkdir TypeScript-SmartContract cd TypeScript-SmartContract
```

Initialize a New Hardhat Project:

You will be guided through setting up your Hardhat environment.

```bash
npx hardhat
```

Choose "Create a sample project" and follow the prompts. This command will create essential files and folders, including a `contracts` folder where we will write our smart contract.

Install Required Dependencies:

In your project directory, install `@nomiclabs/hardhat-ethers` for interacting with contracts.

```bash
npm install --save-dev @nomiclabs/hardhat-ethers ethers
```

Writing the Smart Contract

Now, let's create a simple smart contract. For this example, we will create a contract called `SimpleStorage`, which will store and retrieve a single value.

Navigate to the Contracts Directory:

Inside the `contracts` folder, create a new file called `SimpleStorage.ts`.

Write the Simple Storage Contract:

Here's our SimpleStorage contract in TypeScript:

```typescript
// Import the required libraries import { ethers } from "hardhat";

// We define a simple contract contract SimpleStorage {

// State variable to store a number uint256 private storedData;

// Function to set the value of storedData function set(uint256 x) public {

storedData = x;

}

// Function to get the value of storedData function get() public view returns (uint256) {

return storedData;

}

}
```

Compiling the Smart Contract

To compile the smart contract, run the following command in your terminal:

```bash
npx hardhat compile
```

This command compiles the `SimpleStorage` contract and checks for any syntax or type errors. ## Deploying the Smart Contract

To deploy the smart contract, we will create a deployment script.

Create Deployment Script:

Inside the `scripts` folder, create a new file called `deploy.ts`.

Write the Deployment Logic: Add the following code to `deploy.ts`:

```typescript
import { ethers } from "hardhat";

async function main() {
// Get the contract factory
const SimpleStorage = await ethers.getContractFactory("SimpleStorage");


// Deploy the contract
const simpleStorage = await SimpleStorage.deploy();
// Wait for the deployment to be mined await simpleStorage.deployed();
```

101

```
console.log("SimpleStorage        deployed        to:",
simpleStorage.address);
}
// Run the main function and handle errors
main().catch((error) => {
console.error(error); process.exitCode = 1;
});
```
```

**Deploy to a Local Ethereum Network:** Start a local Ethereum network using Hardhat:

```bash
npx hardhat node
```

In a new terminal tab, deploy the contract:

```bash
npx hardhat run scripts/deploy.ts --network localhost
```

After the deployment is successful, you will see the contract's address in the terminal. ## Interacting with the Deployed Contract

After deploying your smart contract, you can interact with it using scripts or a front-end interface. ### Writing Interaction Commands

Create a new script:

Inside the `scripts` folder, create a file called `interact.ts`.
```

Add Interaction Logic:

In this script, we will call the `set` function to store a value and then retrieve it using the `get` function.

```typescript
import { ethers } from "hardhat";

async function main() {

const addresses = await ethers.getSigners();

const simpleStorageAddress = "YOUR_DEPLOYED_CONTRACT_ADDRESS"; // Replace with your contract's address

// Create a contract instance

const simpleStorage = await ethers.getContractAt("SimpleStorage", simpleStorageAddress);

// Set a value

const setTx = await simpleStorage.connect(addresses[0]).set(42);

await setTx.wait();

// Get the value

const value = await simpleStorage.get();
console.log("Stored value:", value.toString());
}

main().catch((error) => { console.error(error);
process.exitCode = 1;
});
```

Run the Interaction Script:

In your terminal, execute the interaction script:

```bash
npx hardhat run scripts/interact.ts --network localhost
```

We wrote a simple smart contract for storing and retrieving a value, deployed that contract to a local blockchain network, and interacted with it using scripts. As blockchain technology continues to evolve, the need for smart contract developers will only grow, making it an invaluable skill in today's tech landscape.

Chapter 7: Interacting with Smart Contracts Using TypeScript

This chapter will focus on how to interact with these smart contracts using TypeScript, a powerful and widely adopted variant of JavaScript. With its static typing feature, TypeScript enhances code quality and readability, making it an excellent choice for blockchain development.

7.1 Understanding Smart Contracts

Before diving into the practicalities of interaction, let's briefly revisit what smart contracts are. Smart contracts are self-executing contracts with the terms of the agreement directly written into code. They run on blockchain networks, most commonly Ethereum, and are designed to automate processes and reduce the risks associated with traditional contracts.

The main features of smart contracts include:

Automation: Once deployed on the blockchain, smart contracts execute automatically when predetermined conditions are met.

Immutability: Record of transactions and contracts cannot be altered or deleted, ensuring transparency and trust.

Trustless environment: Participants do not need to trust each other, as the contract's code executes the agreed terms.

7.2 Setting Up Your TypeScript Project ### 7.2.1 Prerequisites

Before we start coding, ensure you have Node.js and npm

installed. You will also need to install TypeScript and ethers.js - a library for interacting with the Ethereum blockchain. To get started, create a new directory for the project:

```bash

mkdir smart-contract-interaction cd smart-contract-interaction npm init -y

npm install typescript ts-node ethers @types/node --save-dev

```

7.2.2 Initialize TypeScript

After installing the dependencies, initialize your TypeScript configuration:

```bash

npx tsc --init

```

This will create a `tsconfig.json` file where you can configure TypeScript settings as needed. ## 7.3 Connecting to Ethereum

7.3.1 Setting Up a Provider

To interact with a smart contract, you must connect to the Ethereum network. This is done through a provider. Ethers.js makes this process straightforward. You can use the default provider or configure your own:

```typescript

import { ethers } from "ethers";

```

```typescript
// Choose a provider. Here, we're using the default provider to connect to the Ethereum mainnet. const provider = ethers.getDefaultProvider('homestead');
```

If you want to connect to a test network, like Ropsten or Rinkeby, specify it in the provider:

```typescript
const provider = ethers.getDefaultProvider('ropsten');
```

7.3.2 Loading Wallet Information

Once you have a provider set up, you can connect your wallet to interact with the smart contract. Ensure you have a mnemonic phrase or private key:

```typescript
const privateKey = "your-private-key-here"; // Keep this secure! const wallet = new ethers.Wallet(privateKey, provider);
```

7.4 Interacting with Smart Contracts ### 7.4.1 Contract ABI and Address

To interact with a smart contract, you need its ABI (Application Binary Interface) and the contract address. Assume we are working with a simple ERC20 token contract:

```typescript
const contractAddress = "0xYourContractAddressHere"; const abi = [
```

"function balanceOf(address owner) view returns (uint256)", "function transfer(address to, uint amount) returns (bool)",

];
```

### 7.4.2 Creating a Contract Instance

With the ABI and contract address, you can create a contract instance:

```typescript
const contract = new ethers.Contract(contractAddress, abi, wallet);
```

7.4.3 Reading Data from the Contract

Let's say you want to check the balance of an address:

```typescript
async function getBalance(address: string) {

const balance = await contract.balanceOf(address);
console.log(`Balance: ${ethers.utils.formatUnits(balance, 18)} tokens`);

}
// Call the function with an example address
getBalance("0xExampleAddressHere");
```

7.4.4 Writing Data to the Contract
```

To send a transaction (like transferring tokens), you can call the `transfer` function defined in your contract:

```typescript
async function transferTokens(to: string, amount: string) {

const tx = await contract.transfer(to, ethers.utils.parseUnits(amount, 18)); await tx.wait(); // Wait for the transaction to be mined console.log(`Transferred ${amount} tokens to ${to} successfully.`);

}

// Call the function to transfer tokens transferTokens("0xReceiverAddressHere", "10");
```

7.5 Error Handling

When dealing with async operations, especially with blockchain transactions, error handling is crucial. Wrap your asynchronous calls in try-catch blocks to handle potential errors gracefully:

```typescript
async function safeTransferTokens(to: string, amount: string) { try {

const tx = await contract.transfer(to, ethers.utils.parseUnits(amount, 18)); await tx.wait();

console.log(`Transferred ${amount} tokens to ${to} successfully.`);

} catch (error) {
```

```
console.error("Transaction failed:", error);
}
}
```
` ` `

We explored how to interact with smart contracts on the Ethereum blockchain using TypeScript. We covered setting up our TypeScript project, connecting to the Ethereum network, and performing read and write operations on a smart contract. With TypeScript, the static typing feature allows for better code organization and debugging capabilities.

Using Ethers.js to Communicate with Smart Contracts

Ethers.js is one of the most popular libraries for this purpose, and in this chapter, we will explore how to use Ethers.js in a TypeScript environment to communicate effectively with smart contracts.

What is Ethers.js?

Ethers.js is a library that allows developers to interact with the Ethereum blockchain. It provides a complete and compact interface to work with Ethereum accounts, contracts, and transactions. Ethers.js is designed to be easy to use while also offering significant functionalities, such as encoding and decoding data and managing cryptographic functions.

Key Features of Ethers.js

Lightweight and Compact: Ethers.js is much smaller

than other libraries like web3.js, making it quicker to download and use in browser applications.

TypeScript Support: Ethers.js is written in TypeScript and provides type definitions, making it easier to work with in TypeScript-based projects.

Provider Flexibility: It supports various Ethereum networks (mainnet, testnets) and can connect to local nodes.

Contract Interaction: Easily deploy, read, and write to smart contracts without dealing with intricate low-level details.

Built-in Utilities: It has utilities for tasks such as managing wallets, signing messages, and encoding data for transactions.

Setting Up Your Environment

Before diving into the coding aspect, you need to set up your development environment. Follow these steps:

Install Node.js: Ensure you have Node.js installed on your machine. You can download it from [Node.js official website](https://nodejs.org).

Create a New Project: Use the terminal to create a new directory for your project and navigate into it:

```bash
mkdir ethers-example cd ethers-example
```

Initialize NPM: Initialize a new Node.js project:

```bash npm init -y
```

```
```

Install Ethers.js and TypeScript:
```bash
npm install ethers
npm install typescript ts-node @types/node --save-dev
```

Configure TypeScript: Create a `tsconfig.json` file with basic settings:
```json
{
"compilerOptions": { "target": "ES6", "module": "commonjs", "strict": true, "esModuleInterop": true
},
"include": ["src/**/*"]
}
```

Create your source folder: Create a `src` folder where you will maintain your TypeScript files:
```bash
mkdir src
```

Interacting with a Smart Contract

Now that we have our environment set up, let's interact with a smart contract written in Solidity. For this example, we assume you have a deployed smart contract that has the following functions:

```solidity
pragma solidity ^0.8.0;

contract SimpleStore { uint256 value;

function store(uint256 _value) public { value = _value;
}

function retrieve() public view returns (uint256) { return value;
}

}
```

1. Setting Up the Contract Interface

In your `src` folder, create a new file called `index.ts`. First, we need to define an interface to represent our smart contract:

```typescript
import { ethers } from 'ethers';

// Define the contract's ABI (Application Binary Interface)
const abi = [

"function store(uint256 _value)",

"function retrieve() view returns (uint256)"

];

// Address of the deployed contract

const                    contractAddress              =
"0xYourDeployedContractAddress";
```

2. Connecting to the Ethereum Network

Next, you need to connect to the Ethereum network. For this example, we'll use a test network like Rinkeby. You'll also need an Infura or Alchemy project ID or endpoint URL, along with a wallet provider.

```typescript
async function connectToNetwork() {

const provider = new ethers.providers.InfuraProvider('rinkeby', 'YOUR_INFURA_PROJECT_ID'); return provider;

}
```

3. Creating a Contract Instance

Now, use the provider to create a contract instance, which allows us to call the functions defined in the contract:

```typescript
async function getContract(provider: ethers.providers.Provider) { const contract = new ethers.Contract(contractAddress, abi, provider); return contract;

}
```

4. Reading from the Contract

To read the current value stored in the contract, create a function:

```typescript
```

```typescript
async function readValue() {
```

const provider = await connectToNetwork(); const contract = await getContract(provider); const value = await contract.retrieve(); console.log(`Stored value: ${value.toString()}`);

```
}
```
` ` `

5. Writing to the Contract

To modify the value in the smart contract, we will need a signer (wallet). You'll require a wallet private key and, ideally, some test Ether in your account. Here's how to write to the contract:

` ` `typescript

async function storeValue(value: number) { const provider = await connectToNetwork();

const wallet = new ethers.Wallet('YOUR_WALLET_PRIVATE_KEY', provider); const contract = await getContract(provider.connect(wallet));

const tx = await contract.store(value);

await tx.wait(); // Wait for the transaction to be mined console.log(`Stored value: ${value}`);

```
}
```
` ` `

6. Putting it All Together

Finally, you can create a simple main function to call your read and write methods:

115

````typescript
async function main() {

await storeValue(42); // Store a new value await readValue(); // Retrieve it

}

main().catch(console.error);
````

Running Your Code

You can run your TypeScript code using the following command:

```bash

npx ts-node src/index.ts

```

We covered everything from setting up the environment to reading from and writing to a smart contract. As you develop more complex applications, you can build upon these foundations, incorporating additional tools, frameworks, and best practices from the Ethereum ecosystem.

Fetching Blockchain Data with TypeScript

This chapter will guide you through the process of fetching blockchain data using TypeScript, a popular programming language that brings static typing and more powerful tools to JavaScript.

1. Understanding Blockchain Data

Before diving into code, it's essential to grasp what blockchain data consists of. In essence, blockchain data includes:

Transaction Data: Information about transfers of cryptocurrency or tokens, including sender, receiver, amount, and timestamps.

Block Information: Details regarding individual blocks, including block height, hash, previous hash, and the timestamp of when a block was mined.

Smart Contract Data: Data from decentralized applications (dApps) running on the blockchain.

Types of blockchain networks like Ethereum, Binance Smart Chain, and others may expose their data through various APIs, JSON-RPC interfaces, or directly through peer-to-peer network protocols.

2. Setting Up Your TypeScript Environment

The first step in fetching blockchain data using TypeScript involves setting up a suitable environment. Here's how to get started:

Prerequisites:

Node.js: Ensure you have Node.js installed on your machine. You can download it from nodejs.org.

TypeScript: Install TypeScript globally using npm:

```bash
npm install -g typescript
```

```
```

Project Initialization:

Create a new directory for your project and initialize a new Node.js project:

```bash
mkdir blockchain-data-fetch cd blockchain-data-fetch npm init -y
```

Install TypeScript and the required packages:

```bash
npm install typescript ts-node axios ethers
```

Create a `tsconfig.json` file:

```json
{
"compilerOptions": { "target": "ES6", "module": "commonjs",

"strict": true
},
"include": [ "./src/**/*"
]
}
```

Create a directory for your source code:

```bash
mkdir src
```

3. Fetching Data from Ethereum

Let's take a look at how to fetch data from the Ethereum blockchain using TypeScript. To do this, we will use the `ethers` library, which allows us to interact with the Ethereum network seamlessly.

Writing the Fetch Function

Create a new file `fetchBlockchainData.ts` in the `src` directory and add the following code:

```typescript
import { ethers } from "ethers";

/**
 * Fetches the latest block information from the Ethereum blockchain.
 */
async function fetchLatestBlock() {
// Connect to the Ethereum network (using Infura, Alchemy, or any other provider)
const provider = new ethers.providers.InfuraProvider("mainnet", "YOUR_INFURA_PROJECT_ID");
try {
const latestBlock = await provider.getBlock("latest");
console.log("Latest Block:", latestBlock);
```

```
} catch (error) {

console.error("Error fetching block data:", error);

}

}

fetchLatestBlock();
```

Explanation of the Code

Imports: We import the necessary modules from the `ethers` library.

Provider: We use the `InfuraProvider` to connect to the Ethereum mainnet via Infura. Make sure to replace `"YOUR_INFURA_PROJECT_ID"` with your actual Infura project ID.

Fetching the Block: We call `provider.getBlock("latest")` to retrieve the latest block on the blockchain.

Error Handling: We wrap our fetching process in a try-catch block to handle possible errors gracefully.

Running the Code

To run your TypeScript script, execute the following command in your terminal:

```bash
npx ts-node src/fetchBlockchainData.ts
```

4. Fetching Transaction Data

Now that we can retrieve block data, let's extend our script to fetch transaction data. Replace the content of `fetchBlockchainData.ts` with the following code:

```typescript
import { ethers } from "ethers";
/**
Fetches transaction details by hash from the Ethereum blockchain.
@param txHash - The transaction hash to fetch data for.
*/
async function fetchTransaction(txHash: string) {
const provider = new ethers.providers.InfuraProvider("mainnet", "YOUR_INFURA_PROJECT_ID");
try {
const transaction = await provider.getTransaction(txHash);
console.log("Transaction Details:", transaction);
} catch (error) {
console.error("Error fetching transaction data:", error);
}
}
// Sample transaction hash
const sampleTxHash = "ox5e..."; // Replace with a real transaction hash fetchTransaction(sampleTxHash);
```

Explanation of the Transaction Fetch

We define a new function `fetchTransaction` that takes a transaction hash as an argument.

Using `provider.getTransaction(txHash)`, we fetch the transaction details and log them to the console.

Testing the Transaction Fetch

Replace `const sampleTxHash` with a valid transaction hash from the Ethereum blockchain and run the script again to fetch the transaction details.

Fetching blockchain data with TypeScript allows developers to create robust applications that leverage the decentralized nature of the blockchain. By combining TypeScript's type safety and the power of libraries like ethers.js, you can build applications that are both efficient and easy to maintain.

Chapter 8: Developing Decentralized Applications (dApps) with TypeScript

This chapter explores the unique architecture of dApps, the role of smart contracts, and how to leverage TypeScript to build modern dApps that are not only functional but also maintainable and scalable.

The Architecture of dApps

To understand the development of dApps, it's essential to grasp their architecture, which typically consists of three layers:

Frontend Layer: This is the user-facing part of the application, often built using familiar web technologies like HTML, CSS, and JavaScript/TypeScript.

Smart Contracts Layer: These are self-executing contracts with the terms of the agreement directly written into code. Smart contracts are deployed on a blockchain and manage the logic of the dApp.

Blockchain Layer: This is the underlying infrastructure where the smart contracts are executed and data is stored. Popular blockchain platforms for dApp development include Ethereum, Binance Smart Chain, and others.

Benefits of Using TypeScript for dApp Development

TypeScript is a superset of JavaScript that introduces static typing and advanced features, making it particularly suitable for dApp development. Here are a few reasons why TypeScript should be your go-to language for building dApps:

Strong Typing: TypeScript helps catch errors at compile time, reducing runtime errors and making code more robust.

Enhanced IDE Support: TypeScript's type system provides enhanced code completion and navigation, improving developer productivity.

Improved Readability and Maintainability: With TypeScript, developers can take advantage of interfaces and types, making code easier to understand, especially in larger projects.

Ecosystem Compatibility: TypeScript works seamlessly with existing JavaScript libraries and frameworks, allowing developers to leverage powerful tools like React, Angular, and Vue.js.

Setting Up the Development Environment

To start with dApp development using TypeScript, you'll need to set up your environment. Here's a step-by- step guide:

Prerequisites

Node.js & npm: Install Node.js, which comes with npm (Node Package Manager) to manage your project dependencies.

TypeScript: Install TypeScript globally using npm:

```bash
npm install -g typescript
```

Ethereum Development Framework: For this guide, we'll use Truffle or Hardhat. You can choose one based on your preference:
- **Truffle**:
```bash
npm install -g truffle
```

- **Hardhat**:
```bash
npm install --save-dev hardhat
```

Setting Up a New Project
Create a New Directory:
```bash
mkdir my-dapp cd my-dapp
```

Initialize the Project:
```bash npm init -y
```

Install Required Packages:
For a basic dApp, you will need a few dependencies:
```bash
npm install ethers hardhat --save
npm install @types/node @types/mocha typescript ts-
```

node --save-dev
```

**Create a TypeScript Configuration File**:

Generate a `tsconfig.json` file:

```bash
npx tsc --init
```

Modify the configuration to suit your needs, setting `target` to `es6` or higher and enabling `strict` mode for better type checking.

Basic Project Structure

A recommended project structure for dApps might look like this:

```
/my-dapp
contracts     // Smart contracts MyContract.sol
scripts // Deployment scripts deploy.ts
src     // Frontend source code index.html
app.ts styles.css
tsconfig.json // TypeScript configuration
```

Building Smart Contracts with Solidity

The core logic of your dApp will be captured within smart contracts. In this section, you will learn how to write a simple smart contract using Solidity.
```

Example: A Simple Voting Contract

Create a new file `MyContract.sol` under the `contracts` directory:

```solidity
// SPDX-License-Identifier: MIT pragma solidity ^0.8.0;

contract Voting { struct Candidate {

string name; uint voteCount;

}

mapping(uint => Candidate) public candidates;
mapping(address => bool) public voters;

uint public candidatesCount;

constructor()         {          addCandidate("Alice");
addCandidate("Bob");

}

function addCandidate(string memory name) private {
candidates[candidatesCount] = Candidate(name, 0);
candidatesCount++;

}

function vote(uint candidateIndex) public {
require(!voters[msg.sender], "You have already voted.");

require(candidateIndex < candidatesCount, "Invalid candidate index.");

voters[msg.sender]              =              true;
candidates[candidateIndex].voteCount++;

}

}
```

```
```

Interacting with Smart Contracts in TypeScript

To interact with the deployed smart contract using TypeScript, create a new file called `deploy.ts` under the `scripts` directory. Implement the following code to deploy your smart contract: ### Example: Deploy Script

```typescript
import { ethers } from "hardhat";

async function main() {

const Voting = await ethers.getContractFactory("Voting");
const voting = await Voting.deploy();

console.log("Voting contract deployed to:", voting.address);

}
main()
.then(() => process.exit(0))
.catch((error) => { console.error(error); process.exit(1);
});
```

Compiling and Deploying Your Smart Contract

You can compile your smart contract using Hardhat with the following command:

```bash
npx hardhat compile
```

After compiling successfully, deploy the contract:

```bash
npx hardhat run scripts/deploy.ts --network localhost
```

Make sure you have a local Ethereum node running, or you can use services like Hardhat Network or Ganache.

Building the Frontend

The frontend of your dApp will enable users to interact with the smart contract. Here's a basic example using HTML and TypeScript.

Example: Frontend Structure

index.html: Create a simple UI for voting.

```html
<!DOCTYPE html>
<html lang="en">
<head>
<meta charset="UTF-8">
<meta name="viewport" content="width=device-width, initial-scale=1.0">
<title>Voting dApp</title>
</head>
<body>
<h1>Voting dApp</h1>
```

```html
<div id="candidates"></div>
<script src="app.js"></script>
</body>
</html>
```

app.ts: Write the code to interact with your smart contract.

```typescript
import { ethers } from "ethers";

const provider = new ethers.providers.Web3Provider(window.ethereum); const signer = provider.getSigner();

const votingAddress = "YOUR_VOTING_CONTRACT_ADDRESS"; const votingABI = [

"function candidates(uint256) view returns (string,uint256)", "function candidatesCount() view returns (uint256)", "function vote(uint256)"
];

async function loadCandidates() {

const votingContract = new ethers.Contract(votingAddress, votingABI, signer); const count = await votingContract.candidatesCount();

const candidatesDiv = document.getElementById("candidates"); candidatesDiv.innerHTML = "";
```

```
for (let i = 0; i < count; i++) {
const candidate = await votingContract.candidates(i);
candidatesDiv.innerHTML            +=            `<button
onclick="vote(${i})">${candidate[0]}</button>`;
}
}
async function vote(candidateIndex: number) {
const          votingContract          =          new
ethers.Contract(votingAddress, votingABI, signer); await
votingContract.vote(candidateIndex);
alert("Vote casted!"); loadCandidates();
}
window.onload = loadCandidates;
```

Compiling and Building the Frontend Compile the TypeScript code to JavaScript:

```bash
tsc src/app.ts --outDir dist
```

Ensure that your script tag in `index.html` points to the correct output JavaScript file.

We explored the fundamentals of developing decentralized applications (dApps) using TypeScript. We covered the architecture of dApps, the creation and deployment of smart contracts, and how to build a simple frontend that interacts with our smart contracts.

By using TypeScript, we ensured our code was robust, maintainable, and scalable. As you continue to explore dApp development, you'll discover many advanced topics such as managing state, integrating wallets, and implementing complex user interfaces. With TypeScript and the growing ecosystem of tools, you're well-equipped to navigate the exciting world of decentralized application development.

Further Reading and Resources

[TypeScript Documentation](https://www.typescriptlang.org/docs/)

[Hardhat Documentation](https://hardhat.org/getting-started/)

[Ethereum Smart Contract Development](https://soliditylang.org/docs/)

Structuring a TypeScript-Based dApp

This chapter delves into the essential aspects of structuring a TypeScript-based dApp, combining best practices from both blockchain technology and robust software engineering.

1. Understanding the Components of a dApp

Before diving into the structural aspects, it's crucial to understand what a dApp is composed of. Typically, a dApp involves the following components:

Smart Contracts: Self-executing contracts with the

terms of the agreement directly written into code, deployed on a blockchain.

Frontend: The user interface that interacts with users, often a web application built with JavaScript frameworks like React, Vue, or Angular.

Backend: While dApps can be largely decentralized, a backend may still be required to handle specific tasks, such as off-chain data storage or processing, normally built with Node.js.

Blockchain Network: The underlying blockchain technology that supports the dApp, such as Ethereum, Binance Smart Chain, or Polygon.

Understanding these components helps in structuring the application effectively. ## 2. Setting Up the Development Environment

To start building a TypeScript-based dApp, you need a solid development environment:

Node.js and npm: Ensure you have Node.js installed, as it allows you to run JavaScript on the server side. npm comes bundled with Node.js and helps manage project dependencies.

TypeScript: Install TypeScript globally using npm:

```bash
npm install -g typescript
```

Framework Selection: Choose a frontend framework that supports TypeScript. React, for example, works seamlessly with TypeScript:

```bash
npx create-react-app my-dapp --template typescript
```

Solidity & Truffle/Hardhat: For smart contract development:

- Install Truffle:
```bash
npm install -g truffle
```

- Or install Hardhat:
```bash
npm install --save-dev hardhat
```

Web3 Libraries: Choose libraries like Ethers.js or Web3.js to interact with the Ethereum blockchain:
```bash
npm install ethers
```

3. Project Structure

Structuring a TypeScript-based dApp efficiently promotes clarity and efficiency in both development and maintenance. Here's a suggested project structure:

```plaintext my-dapp/
```

```
contracts/      # Smart contracts directory MyContract.sol
Migrations.sol


src/    # Main source directory components/
        # React components hooks/           # Custom
React hooks
utils/ # Utility functions
types/ # Type definitions
App.tsx         # Main application file index.tsx  #      Entry
point for React app


scripts/        # Deployment scripts deploy.ts


test/   # Smart contract tests MyContract.test.ts
helper.ts


.env    # Environment variables

.gitignore      # Git ignore rules hardhat.config.ts
        # Hardhat configuration

package.json            # NPM package management file
tsconfig.json # TypeScript configuration
```
```

### 3.1 Contracts Directory

The contracts directory houses all your smart contracts
written in Solidity. Each contract should be modular and
```

focused on specific functionality. Adopt a naming convention that reflects the contract's purpose, aiding in both readability and discoverability.

3.2 Source Directory

The source directory typically contains all frontend-related code. Utilizing TypeScript's interfaces and types in this part of your application can greatly reduce bugs and improve clarity, particularly when dealing with blockchain data structures or API responses.

3.3 Scripts Directory

Deployment scripts are essential for automating the process of deploying your contracts to the blockchain. Each script should be well-documented, explaining the functionalities and dependencies.

3.4 Test Directory

Testing is essential, especially in blockchain applications where bugs can lead to significant financial loss. Follow the Test-Driven Development (TDD) process to write your tests in TypeScript, focusing on both contract-level tests (using frameworks like Mocha/Chai) and end-to-end tests for your dApp.

4. Implementing Smart Contracts with TypeScript Types

Integrate TypeScript types with your smart contracts to help ensure type safety throughout your dApp. Create TypeScript interfaces representing the desired structures of your smart contracts, which can be useful for interacting with them via your frontend.

Example:

```typescript
// types/MyContract.ts

export interface MyContract { owner(): Promise<string>;

setValue(value: number): Promise<void>; getValue():
Promise<number>;

}
```

Additionally, utilize libraries that generate TypeScript definitions from your smart contracts, such as TypeChain, to streamline interactions.

5. Interacting with the Blockchain

Once you've structured your codebase and implemented your smart contracts, interacting with the blockchain is the next critical step. The wallet integration (ex: MetaMask) is pivotal, and Ethers.js provides a user-friendly interface for connecting wallets and calling smart contract methods.

Example of Contract Interaction:

```typescript
import { ethers } from "ethers";

import { MyContract } from "./types/MyContract";

async function getContract() {

const              provider              =              new
ethers.providers.Web3Provider(window.ethereum);   //
Assuming  user  has  MetaMask  const  signer  =
provider.getSigner();
```

```
// Example contract address

const contractAddress = "oxYourContractAddress";

const contract = new ethers.Contract(contractAddress,
contractABI, signer) as MyContract; return contract;

}

async function readValue() {

const contract = await getContract(); const value = await
contract.getValue();

console.log("Value from contract:", value);

}


```
```

6. Testing and Deployment

Testing is crucial for ensuring that your smart contracts and your dApp's frontend work seamlessly. Use frameworks like Mocha and Chai to write your tests for smart contracts, and for the frontend, leverage tools like Jest or React Testing Library.

When deploying your dApps, consider using tools like Infura or Alchemy for accessing blockchain networks. Deploy your smart contracts to a test network (e.g., Rinkeby or Ropsten) before moving to the mainnet.

By understanding the components of dApps, setting up a robust development environment, structuring the project effectively, and leveraging TypeScript's strengths, you can create scalable, maintainable, and efficient decentralized applications. As the blockchain landscape continues to
```

evolve, the ability to adapt and innovate will remain paramount for developers venturing into this exciting field.

Connecting Frontend and Backend Using Web3.js & TypeScript

This chapter will delve into the connection between the frontend and backend of a dApp using Web3.js and TypeScript, two powerful tools that enhance development efficiency and maintainability.

Understanding the Basics ### What is Web3.js?

Web3.js is a JavaScript library that allows you to interact with the Ethereum blockchain. It acts as a bridge between your frontend application and the Ethereum network, enabling developers to read blockchain data, send transactions, and interact with smart contracts. The library provides an abstraction layer that simplifies the complexity involved in using the Ethereum JSON-RPC interface.

Why TypeScript?

TypeScript, a superset of JavaScript, introduces static typing and enhances code quality through better tooling and error checking. By using TypeScript, we can catch potential errors at compile time rather than at runtime, leading to more robust and maintainable code. Furthermore, TypeScript's interface and type definition features enhance our interaction with Web3.js, allowing for a more structured approach to managing data.

Setting Up the Project

To effectively connect the frontend and backend, we will create a simple project structure. The primary tools we'll need are Node.js, npm (or yarn), and a development environment such as Visual Studio Code.

Step 1: Initialize the Project

First, create a new directory for your project and initialize it:

```bash
mkdir my-dapp cd my-dapp npm init -y
```

Step 2: Install Dependencies

Next, install the necessary packages, including TypeScript, Web3.js, and the necessary typings:

```bash
npm install web3

npm install typescript @types/node @types/web3 --save-dev
```

After installing the packages, we will also need to initialize TypeScript configuration:

```bash
npx tsc --init
```

This command will create a `tsconfig.json` file, where we can specify our compiler options. ### Step 3: Create

Project Structure

Organizing your project structure is crucial for maintainability:

```
```

my-dapp/ src/

index.ts contract.ts web3.ts

package.json tsconfig.json

```
```

Connecting Frontend to Backend ### Setting Up Web3 Provider

The first step in connecting your frontend to the Ethereum network is to configure Web3.js to use an Ethereum provider. This can be either a local node or a service such as Infura or Alchemy.

In `web3.ts`, configure the Web3 provider as follows:

```typescript
import Web3 from 'web3';

const provider = (window as any).ethereum || 'http://localhost:8545'; const web3 = new Web3(provider);

export default web3;
```

Interacting with Smart Contracts

Smart contracts are the backbone of any dApp. To interact with them, you'll need their ABI (Application Binary Interface) and contract address.

141

In `contract.ts`, you can create a function that sets up your contract instance:

```typescript
import web3 from './web3';

const contractABI = [...]; // Your smart contract ABI const contractAddress = '0xYourContractAddress';

const contract = new web3.eth.Contract(contractABI, contractAddress); export default contract;
```

Creating Functions to Call Blockchain Methods

Now, let's create functions to interact with the smart contract. For example, you might want to read a value from the contract or send a transaction to update it.

In `contract.ts`, add the following functions:

```typescript
export const getValue = async () => {

const value = await contract.methods.yourMethod().call();
return value;

};

export const setValue = async (newValue: string) => {
const accounts = await web3.eth.getAccounts();

await contract.methods.yourMethod(newValue).send({
from: accounts[0] });

};
```

Integrating with the Frontend

142

With the backend and contract interaction set up, it's time to integrate these functionalities into the frontend. In `index.ts`, we'll create a simple user interface.

```typescript
import web3 from './web3';

import { getValue, setValue } from './contract'; const app = document.getElementById('app');

const loadData = async () => { const value = await getValue();

app.innerHTML = `<h1>Current Value: ${value}</h1>`;

};

const updateValue = async () => {

const newValue = (document.getElementById('newValue') as HTMLInputElement).value; await setValue(newValue);

loadData();

};

// Event listener for button document.getElementById('updateButton').addEventListener('click', updateValue);

// Initial load loadData();
```

Example HTML Structure

You will need a simple HTML structure to host your application:

```html
<!DOCTYPE html>
```

```html
<html lang="en">
<head>
<meta charset="UTF-8">
<meta name="viewport" content="width=device-width,
initial-scale=1.0">
<title>My dApp</title>
</head>
<body>
<div id="app"></div>
<input type="text" id="newValue" placeholder="Enter
new value" />
<button id="updateButton">Update Value</button>
<script src="dist/index.js"></script>
</body>
</html>
```

By leveraging TypeScript's static typing and Web3.js's robust functionality, developers can create efficient and maintainable dApps. As you continue to enhance your project, consider implementing additional features like user authentication, wallet integration, and network error handling.

Chapter 9: Handling Blockchain Transactions Securely

In this chapter, we will explore the best practices, tools, and libraries useful for handling blockchain transactions securely in TypeScript. We'll dive into the principles of secure coding, transaction validation, and various cryptographic techniques that underpin secure blockchain operations.

1. Understanding Blockchain Transactions ### 1.1 Basics of Blockchain Transactions

A blockchain transaction is a digital representation of an agreement between parties. When we talk about blockchain transactions, we are primarily concerned with:

Signing: Ensuring that the transaction is authorized by the sender through cryptographic signatures.

Broadcasting: Sending the transaction to the network for validation and inclusion in a block.

Confirmation: Achieving consensus among nodes that the transaction is valid and should be added to the blockchain.

1.2 Importance of Security in Transactions

The primary goal of handling blockchain transactions securely is to prevent unauthorized access, manipulation, and fraud. Security compromises can lead to severe financial losses and damage to reputation. Protecting sensitive data, access controls, and maintaining integrity are foundational to the security of any blockchain system.

2. Setting Up Your TypeScript Environment

To handle blockchain transactions securely in TypeScript, we need to set up our development environment. Here's a brief rundown of the necessary tools:

2.1 Requirements

Node.js: Make sure you have Node.js installed, as it provides the runtime environment for our TypeScript code.

TypeScript: Install TypeScript globally using npm:

```bash
npm install -g typescript
```

Web3.js or Ethers.js: These libraries enable interaction with the Ethereum blockchain. Choose one based on your requirements.

2.2 Installing Libraries

You can install libraries like Web3.js or Ethers.js directly into your project:

```bash
npm install ethers
```

Or if using Web3.js:

```bash
npm install web3
```

3. Implementing Secure Transactions ### 3.1 Creating a Secure Wallet

A blockchain wallet is a container for public and private keys. Here, we will create a simple wallet using the Ethers.js library.

```typescript
import { Wallet, utils } from 'ethers';

const createWallet = () => {

const wallet = Wallet.createRandom();
console.log(`Address: ${wallet.address}`);
console.log(`Private Key: ${wallet.privateKey}`); return wallet;

};

const myWallet = createWallet();
```

3.2 Signing Transactions

Before broadcasting a transaction, it needs to be signed with the private key of the wallet. This step ensures that only the owner can authorize the spend.

```typescript
const signTransaction = async (wallet: Wallet, transaction: any) => { const signedTransaction = await wallet.signTransaction(transaction); return signedTransaction;

};
```

3.3 Broadcasting Transactions

After signing the transaction, the next step is to send it to

147

the blockchain network.

```typescript
const sendTransaction = async (signedTransaction: string,
provider: any) => { const transactionResponse = await
provider.sendTransaction(signedTransaction);
console.log(`Transaction                          Hash:
${transactionResponse.hash}`);

await                          transactionResponse.wait();
console.log('Transaction confirmed!');
};
```

4. Ensuring Integrity and Security

4.1 Using Nonce to Prevent Replay Attacks

A nonce is a unique number that ensures that old
transactions cannot be replayed to the blockchain
network. When creating a transaction, always increment
the nonce.


```typescript
const getNonce = async (walletAddress: string, provider:
any)       =>       {       const       nonce       =       await
provider.getTransactionCount(walletAddress);       return
nonce;
};
```

4.2 Implementing Rate Limiting

148

To prevent abuse of transaction broadcasting, implement rate limiting on your APIs. This can be done with libraries like `express-rate-limit`.

4.3 Transaction Validation

Before sending a transaction, validate its parameters thoroughly:

Ensure correct format of addresses.

Validate gas price and gas limit.

Check if the sender has enough balance.

```typescript
const validateTransaction = (transaction: any) => { if (!utils.isAddress(transaction.to)) {

throw new Error('Invalid recipient address');

}

// Further validations...

};
```

By leveraging TypeScript and libraries such as Ethers.js or Web3.js, developers can create robust and secure applications that interact with blockchain networks. As you proceed with your journey in blockchain development, remember to stay informed about the latest security best practices and continuously audit your code for vulnerabilities.

Signing and Sending Transactions with TypeScript

This chapter will delve into how to leverage TypeScript, a strongly typed superset of JavaScript, to sign and send transactions effectively while ensuring type safety and error handling.

Understanding Transactions

Before we dive into the mechanics, it's essential to understand the basic concepts of a blockchain transaction:

Transaction Structure: A typical blockchain transaction consists of several components, including sender and receiver addresses, value to be transferred, fees, and any additional data if required by the network.

Signing: Signing a transaction involves cryptographic functions that ensure authenticity and integrity. A private key generates a unique signature that proves ownership of the assets involved in a transaction.

Broadcasting: Once a transaction is signed, it needs to be sent (or broadcast) to the network, where miners or validators will process and include it in a new block.

Setting Up the Environment

Before we start writing our TypeScript code, we need to set up our development environment. Ensure you have the following:

Node.js installed on your computer.

A code editor such as Visual Studio Code.

TypeScript installed. This can be done using npm:

```bash
npm install -g typescript
```

Necessary libraries related to blockchain interactions, commonly used libraries include `ethers.js` for Ethereum and `bitcoinjs-lib` for Bitcoin transactions.

Installing Required Libraries

For this chapter, we will use `ethers.js`, a comprehensive library for interacting with the Ethereum blockchain. Install it using npm:

```bash
npm install ethers
```

Signing Transactions with TypeScript

To begin, let's first explore how to sign a transaction using `ethers.js` in TypeScript. The following steps outline the process:

Import Libraries: Start by importing the necessary modules from the library.

Create a Wallet: You'll need to create a wallet using your private key. In a real application, ensure that sensitive data like your private key is handled securely.

Define the Transaction: Create a transaction object, which includes details like nonce, gas price, and data.

Sign the Transaction: Use the wallet object to sign the transaction.

Here's how you can wrap these steps in TypeScript code:

```typescript
import { ethers } from 'ethers';

// Replace with your own private key (keep this private!)
const privateKey = 'YOUR_PRIVATE_KEY_HERE'; const
wallet = new ethers.Wallet(privateKey);

// Define transaction details const tx = {

to: 'RECEIVER_ADDRESS_HERE',

value: ethers.utils.parseEther('0.01'), // amount in Ether
gasLimit: 21000, // gas limit

gasPrice: ethers.utils.parseUnits('20', 'gwei'), // gas price

nonce: 0 // nones should be fetched from your wallet or
blockchain

};

// Sign the transaction

async function signTransaction(transaction: any) {

const        signedTx        =        await
wallet.signTransaction(transaction); console.log('Signed
Transaction:', signedTx);

}

//        Call        the        sign        function
signTransaction(tx).catch(console.error);
```

Handling Errors

Always ensure to handle potential errors, especially
involving network calls and cryptographic functions. You

can do this using try/catch blocks and proper error messaging.

```typescript
async function signTransaction(transaction: any) { try {

const          signedTx          =          await wallet.signTransaction(transaction); console.log('Signed Transaction:', signedTx);

} catch (error) {

console.error('Error signing transaction:', error);

}

}
```

Sending Transactions to the Blockchain

After successfully signing the transaction, the next step is to send it to the blockchain network. Here's how to do it using `ethers.js`:

```typescript
async function sendTransaction(signedTx: string) {

const provider = ethers.getDefaultProvider('rinkeby'); // Use your desired Ethereum network const txResponse = await provider.sendTransaction(signedTx);

console.log('Transaction Response:', txResponse);

}

// Modify signTransaction function to send the transaction after signing async function
```

```
signAndSendTransaction(transaction: any) {

try {

const        signedTx        =        await
wallet.signTransaction(transaction);  console.log('Signed
Transaction:', signedTx);

await sendTransaction(signedTx);

} catch (error) { console.error('Error:', error);

}

}
```
` ` `

Conclusion

In this chapter, we explored the process of signing and sending transactions using TypeScript and the ethers.js library within the context of blockchain technology. Understanding how to programmatically handle transactions provides developers with the tools to build sophisticated dApps and integrate blockchain capabilities into their applications. As you continue to learn about blockchain development, remember to prioritize security, especially when dealing with private keys and sensitive data.

Testing on Testnets: Experiment with test networks like Rinkeby or Ropsten to practice without using real Ether.

Transaction Monitoring: Implement features that allow monitoring of transaction status and confirmations.

Building dApps: Use these skills to develop full-fledged decentralized applications that interact with the

Ethereum blockchain.

By leveraging TypeScript and libraries like ethers.js, you can create robust and secure blockchain applications that are not only effective but also maintain high standards of code quality and maintainability.

Implementing Security Best Practices for Web3 Transactions

Implementing security best practices in TypeScript—a popular language for building robust Web3 applications—ensures that developers can create secure systems that users can rely on. This chapter discusses key security practices to adopt when implementing Web3 transactions in TypeScript.

Understanding Web3 Security Challenges

Before diving into implementation strategies, it's crucial to understand the common security challenges faced in Web3 environments:

Smart Contract Vulnerabilities: Issues such as reentrancy attacks, gas limit manipulations, and improper access controls.

Phishing Attacks: Users may fall victim to malicious websites mimicking legitimate applications.

Data Deviation: Unauthorized access to private keys or sensitive information.

Transaction Replay: Attackers can reuse transactions on different chains if not carefully handled.

Untrusted Oracles: Reliance on external data sources

can introduce risks if these sources are compromised.

Best Practices for Securing Web3 Transactions ### 1. Employ Comprehensive Testing and Auditing

Before deploying any smart contract, it's essential to conduct thorough testing, including unit tests, integration tests, and formal verification. Adopting TypeScript brings in type checking, which helps catch bugs early.

```typescript
import { ethers, waffle } from 'hardhat'; import { expect } from 'chai';

describe('MyToken', function () { let myToken: MyToken;

beforeEach(async function () {

const        MyTokenFactory        =        await ethers.getContractFactory('MyToken'); myToken = await MyTokenFactory.deploy();

await myToken.deployed();

});

it('should correctly mint tokens', async function () { await myToken.mint(addr1.address, 100);

expect(await myToken.balanceOf(addr1.address)).to.equal(100);

});

// Add more test cases...

});
```

2. Use Secure Libraries and Frameworks

Utilize tried-and-tested libraries such as OpenZeppelin for smart contract development. These libraries have been rigorously audited and provide a secure foundation for your contracts.

```typescript
import { ERC20 } from '@openzeppelin/contracts/token/ERC20/ERC20.sol';

contract MyToken is ERC20 {

constructor() ERC20("My Token", "MTK") {

_mint(msg.sender, 1000000 * 10 ** decimals());

}

}
```

3. Establish Access Control

Implement proper access control mechanisms to ensure only authorized users can execute sensitive operations. Use modifiers to enforce restrictions on functions.

```typescript
import { OpenZeppelin } from '@openzeppelin/contracts/access/Ownable.sol';

contract MyContract is Ownable {

function restrictedFunction() public onlyOwner {

// functionality that only the owner can execute

}

}
```

```
```

4. Use Environment Variables for Secrets

Store sensitive information, such as private keys and API keys, in environment variables instead of hardcoding them into the application.

```typescript
import dotenv from 'dotenv'; dotenv.config();

const privateKey = process.env.PRIVATE_KEY; const mnemonic = process.env.MNEMONIC;
```

5. Implement Proper Error Handling

Gracefully handle errors and rejections, especially with promises, to ensure sensitive data does not leak and users clearly understand the issues. TypeScript's type system can help identify potential issues early on.

```typescript
async function executeTransaction(transaction: Transaction): Promise<void> { try {

await blockchainService.sendTransaction(transaction);

} catch (error) {

console.error('Transaction failed:', error.message);


}
}
```

6. Monitor and Log Activities

Establish logging mechanisms to monitor transaction activities. Use libraries like Winston to create logs that can help trace issues later on.

```typescript
import { createLogger, transports, format } from 'winston';

const logger = createLogger({ level: 'info',

format: format.json(), transports: [

new transports.Console(),

new transports.File({ filename: 'transaction.log' }),

],

});

logger.info('Transaction executed', { transactionId: '12345' });
```

7. Use Multi-Signature Wallets for Important Transactions

Implement multi-signature wallets to enhance security. This requires multiple private keys to sign a transaction before it is executed.

```typescript
// Assuming multi-signature logic is implemented in a smart contract contract MultiSigWallet {

function confirmTransaction(uint transactionId) public onlyOwners {

// Logic for confirming transaction
```

159

```
}
}
```

8. Encourage User Education

Educate users about Web3 security, including the risks of phishing, secure wallet management, and recognizing suspicious activities. Building a comprehensive resource library on security can go a long way.

9. Implement Rate Limiting and Monitoring

To protect against DoS attacks, implement rate limiting on incoming requests. Use middleware in your application to control the number of requests from a single user.

```typescript
import rateLimit from 'express-rate-limit';

const apiLimiter = rateLimit({

windowMs: 15 * 60 * 1000, // 15 minutes

max: 100, // limit each IP to 100 requests per windowMs

);

app.use('/api/', apiLimiter);
```

By leveraging TypeScript, developers can enhance security protocols, reduce vulnerabilities, and create more robust decentralized applications. Awareness and vigilance in every aspect—coding, testing, and user education—are crucial pillars in establishing a safe environment for Web3 transactions.

Chapter 10: Unit Testing and Debugging Smart Contracts in TypeScript

This chapter explores how to implement unit testing and debugging for smart contracts using TypeScript, which has gained popularity due to its static typing and modern features.

Understanding Smart Contract Development

Before we delve into unit testing and debugging, it's essential to understand the fundamentals of smart contracts. Smart contracts are typically written in languages such as Solidity or Vyper for Ethereum-based blockchains. The development process often involves:

Writing the Smart Contract: The smart contract code is developed, generally containing the logic for the decentralized application.

Compiling the Code: The code is compiled to bytecode that can be deployed on the blockchain.

Deployment: The compiled code is deployed to the blockchain, making it accessible for users and other contracts.

Interactivity: Once deployed, users can interact with the smart contract through transactions.

However, because these interactions are immutable, mistakes in the smart contract code can be costly. Therefore, comprehensive testing and debugging processes are critical.

The Importance of Unit Testing

Unit testing is a software testing method by which individual units of source code, including smart contracts, are tested to determine if they are fit for use. Some reasons why unit testing is essential for smart contracts include:

Identifying Bugs Early: Unit tests can help catch bugs before the code is deployed, significantly reducing the risk of severe issues arising in production.

Ensuring Code Quality: Tests act as documentation for the expected behavior of the contract. They enforce correctness and can prevent future changes from breaking existing features.

Improving Developer Confidence: A well-tested smart contract provides assurance to developers and stakeholders that the code behaves as intended.

Setting Up the Testing Environment

To set up a testing environment for smart contracts using TypeScript, you need a few essential components:

Node.js: Ensure you have Node.js installed, as it will allow you to run JavaScript and TypeScript applications.

TypeScript: Install TypeScript globally using npm:

```bash
npm install -g typescript
```

Testing Framework: Popular testing frameworks for Ethereum development include Mocha and Chai. You can install these packages with npm:

```bash
```

```bash
npm install --save-dev mocha chai
```

Ethereum Testing Library: Libraries like Hardhat or Truffle can be used to streamline the deployment and testing of smart contracts. To use Hardhat, install it with:

```bash
npm install --save-dev hardhat
```

Smart Contract Framework: You will also need to install a framework like `ethers.js` or `web3.js` to interact with your smart contracts. For instance:

```bash
npm install ethers
```

Writing Unit Tests in TypeScript

Once your environment is set up, you can proceed to write unit tests for your smart contracts. Below is a basic workflow to write a unit test for a smart contract.

Example Smart Contract

Consider a simple ERC20 token smart contract written in Solidity:

```solidity
// SimpleToken.sol pragma solidity ^0.8.0;
contract SimpleToken {
```

```solidity
string public name = "SimpleToken"; string public symbol = "STK";

uint8 public decimals = 18; uint256 public totalSupply;

mapping(address => uint256) public balanceOf;
constructor(uint256 initialSupply) {

totalSupply = initialSupply * (10 ** uint256(decimals));

balanceOf[msg.sender] = totalSupply;

}

function transfer(address to, uint256 amount) public {
require(balanceOf[msg.sender] >= amount, "Insufficient balance"); balanceOf[msg.sender] -= amount;

balanceOf[to] += amount;

}
}
```

Creating Unit Tests

Now, let's create TypeScript tests using Hardhat and Mocha. Create a file named `SimpleToken.test.ts` in your `test` directory:

```typescript
// SimpleToken.test.ts

import { ethers } from "hardhat";


import { expect } from "chai";
describe("SimpleToken", function () { let simpleToken:
```

```javascript
any;
beforeEach(async function () {
  const SimpleToken = await
  ethers.getContractFactory("SimpleToken"); simpleToken
  = await SimpleToken.deploy(1000);
  await simpleToken.deployed();
});
it("Should have the correct name and symbol", async
function () { expect(await
simpleToken.name()).to.equal("SimpleToken");
expect(await simpleToken.symbol()).to.equal("STK");
});
it("Should assign the total supply to the owner", async
function () { const [owner] = await ethers.getSigners();
  expect(await
  simpleToken.balanceOf(owner.address)).to.equal(1000 *
  (10 ** 18));
});
it("Should transfer tokens between accounts", async
function () { const [owner, addr1] = await
ethers.getSigners();
  await simpleToken.transfer(addr1.address, 50);
  expect(await
  simpleToken.balanceOf(owner.address)).to.equal(950 *
  (10 ** 18)); expect(await
  simpleToken.balanceOf(addr1.address)).to.equal(50);
});
```

```
it("Should fail if sender doesn't have enough tokens",
async function () { const [owner, addr1] = await
ethers.getSigners();

await
expect(simpleToken.connect(addr1).transfer(owner.addre
ss, 50))

.to.be.revertedWith("Insufficient balance");

});

});
```

Running Tests

To run your tests, execute the following command in your terminal:

```bash
npx hardhat test
```

This command will compile your contracts and run the tests defined in your test files. If all goes well, you should see output indicating that your tests have passed.

Debugging Smart Contracts

While unit testing helps catch many issues, debugging is equally important. Debugging smart contracts can be particularly challenging due to the nature of blockchain technology, where transactions can be costly, and smart contract behavior can be non-intuitive.

Tools for Debugging

Hardhat Debugger: Hardhat provides powerful debugging tools that allow you to step through your code, inspect states, and analyze transactions. You can enable debugging by using the `hardhat console` command.

Remix IDE: Remix is an online IDE that supports Solidity smart contract development. It features integrated debugging tools, allowing you to deploy and debug contracts directly in the browser.

Tracing Transactions: Blockchain explorers like Etherscan allow you to trace transactions and view the state changes triggered by smart contracts.

Best Practices in Testing and Debugging

To maximize the effectiveness of your unit testing and debugging processes, consider the following best practices:

Write Tests Early and Often: Incorporate testing into your workflow from the beginning. Write tests for every new feature or change to existing functionality.

Use Descriptive Test Names: Clearly describe what each test is validating to make it easier for others (and yourself) to understand the purpose of the tests.

Test Edge Cases: Implement tests for edge cases and invalid inputs to ensure your smart contracts can handle unexpected situations gracefully.

Keep Tests Independent: Each test should be self-contained and independent from others to avoid cascading failures.

Automate Testing: Automate your testing process to run tests regularly, especially before deploying to production environments.

Unit testing and debugging are essential components of developing reliable smart contracts. By leveraging TypeScript alongside powerful testing frameworks, developers can ensure their smart contracts are robust, secure, and function as intended.

Writing Unit Tests for Smart Contracts Using Chai & Mocha

Because they often handle significant financial transactions on decentralized platforms, ensuring their correctness with rigorous testing is critical.

In this chapter, we will explore how to effectively write unit tests for smart contracts using two popular JavaScript testing frameworks, Chai and Mocha, within a TypeScript environment. This combination will not only leverage TypeScript's strong typing features for better code quality but will also utilize Chai's expressive assertion library and Mocha's flexible test structure to create comprehensive unit tests.

Setting Up Your Development Environment

Before we dive into writing tests, let's ensure we have the necessary tools and setup:

Node.js and npm: Make sure you have Node.js installed on your machine. You can verify it by running `node -v` and `npm -v` in your terminal.

Truffle or Hardhat: For this chapter, we will use Hardhat, a powerful development environment for Ethereum applications. To set up a new project, run the following commands:

```bash
mkdir my-smart-contracts cd my-smart-contracts npm
init -y

npm install --save-dev hardhat npx hardhat
```

Select "Create an empty hardhat.config.js" when
prompted.

Install TypeScript and Necessary Dependencies: Run
the following commands to install TypeScript and typings
for Chai and Mocha:

```bash
npm install --save-dev typescript ts-node @types/node
@types/mocha @types/chai chai mocha ethereum- waffle
```

Configure TypeScript: Create a `tsconfig.json` file in
your project root with the following configuration:

```json
{

"compilerOptions": { "target": "ES2020", "module":
"commonjs", "outDir": "./dist", "strict": true,
"esModuleInterop": true,

"skipLibCheck": true

},

"include": ["./scripts", "./test", "./contracts"], "exclude":
["node_modules"]
```

```
}
```

Install Hardhat EVM: For testing smart contracts, install the Ethereum Waffle plugin:

```bash
npm install --save-dev hardhat-waffle @nomiclabs/hardhat-ethers ethers
```

Writing a Simple Smart Contract

Let's create a simple smart contract for demonstration. Create a new file in the `contracts` directory named `SimpleStorage.sol`:

```solidity
// SPDX-License-Identifier: MIT pragma solidity ^0.8.0;
contract SimpleStorage { uint256 private storedData;
function set(uint256 x) public { storedData = x;
}
function get() public view returns (uint256) { return storedData;
}
}
```

This contract allows you to set and retrieve a simple integer value. ## Writing Unit Tests with Chai & Mocha

Now that we have our smart contract, it's time to write

unit tests. Create a new file in the `test` directory named `SimpleStorage.test.ts`.

```typescript
import { expect } from "chai"; import { ethers } from
"hardhat"; import { Contract } from "ethers";

describe("SimpleStorage", function () { let simpleStorage:
Contract;

beforeEach(async function () {

const        SimpleStorage        =        await
ethers.getContractFactory("SimpleStorage");
simpleStorage = await SimpleStorage.deploy();

await simpleStorage.deployed();

});

it("Should start with a stored value of 0", async function ()
{ expect(await simpleStorage.get()).to.equal(0);

});

it("Should update the stored value", async function () {
await simpleStorage.set(42);

expect(await simpleStorage.get()).to.equal(42);

});

it("Should allow updating the stored value multiple
times", async function () { await simpleStorage.set(10);

await simpleStorage.set(20);

expect(await simpleStorage.get()).to.equal(20);

});

});
```

```

```

Explanation of the Test Code

Import Statements: We import `expect` from Chai for assertions and the `ethers` library from Hardhat for contract interaction.

Describe Block: We define a test suite with `describe`, providing a clear context for the tests it contains.

Before Each Hook: The `beforeEach` function ensures that a fresh instance of the `SimpleStorage` contract is deployed before each test. This isolates the tests and ensures consistent states.

Test Cases:

The first test checks that the initial value is `0`.

The second test verifies that setting the value updates it correctly.

The third test checks that multiple updates function correctly and the final value is as expected. ## Running the Tests

To run the tests, you can execute the following command in your terminal:

```bash
npx hardhat test
```

This command will compile your contracts and execute the test cases defined in `SimpleStorage.test.ts`. You should see an output indicating that all tests have passed.

By utilizing these tools, developers can ensure their smart

contracts perform as expected, reducing the risk of bugs and vulnerabilities.

Debugging Common Issues in TypeScript-Based Blockchain Apps

In this chapter, we will explore common issues developers encounter while building TypeScript-based blockchain applications and provide effective debugging strategies to resolve them.

Understanding the Blockchain Ecosystem

Before diving into debugging, it's crucial to establish a foundational understanding of blockchain applications. These applications often involve interacting with smart contracts, managing on-chain data, and handling decentralized identities. The asynchronous nature of blockchain transactions can introduce unique bugs and challenges, making debugging critical.

Common Issues in TypeScript Blockchain Apps ### 1. Type Mismatches

TypeScript's primary advantage is its strong typing; however, this can lead to type mismatches when interfacing with blockchain data. Often, the returned data from a contract or an SDK may not match the expected TypeScript types, leading to runtime errors.

Debugging Strategy:

Use Type Assertion: When calling functions that return dynamic data, use type assertions carefully to inform TypeScript about the expected structure.

Interface Definitions: Define interfaces that reflect the blockchain entities. This approach helps catch errors during compile time rather than runtime.

2. Asynchronous Errors

Blockchain interactions are inherently asynchronous, and improperly handled promises can lead to unexpected application behavior or unhandled promise rejections.

Debugging Strategy:

Async/Await: Utilize async/await syntax to improve readability and manage flows better. Always use try/catch blocks around await calls to handle errors.

Promise.all: When making multiple calls, use `Promise.all()` to handle multiple promises effectively. Ensure you account for rejection scenarios to maintain app stability.

3. Gas Limit and Transaction Failures

When dealing with Ethereum (or similar) smart contracts, developers often encounter issues related to gas limits and transaction failures. These can result from insufficient gas being provided or incorrect transaction parameters.

Debugging Strategy:

Estimate Gas: Use tools such as Web3.js or Ethers.js to estimate gas required before sending a transaction.

Transaction Logs: Make use of transaction logs and events to debug what happens during the execution of your smart contract.

4. Dependency Issues

TypeScript projects often depend on several third-party libraries, which can introduce conflicts or be outdated. This is particularly true in the rapidly evolving blockchain ecosystem.

Debugging Strategy:

Check Versions: Use tools like npm or yarn to check for the latest compatibility between libraries. Always lock dependency versions in `package.json`.

Peer Dependencies: Pay attention to peer dependencies. When upgrading libraries, ensure that other libraries in your project still support the relevant versions.

5. Network Configuration and Connection Issues

Configuring network settings incorrectly, such as provider URLs, can lead to issues in blockchain-based applications.

Debugging Strategy:

Environment Configuration: Use environment variables to dynamically set configuration for different networks (development, staging, production).

Testing with Local Nodes: Start with a local blockchain setup (like Ganache) for development, which allows for faster feedback and easier debugging.

6. State Management Errors

Managing state – whether local or on-chain – can introduce subtle bugs. Issues can arise when local state does not accurately reflect the on-chain state.

Debugging Strategy:

Event Listeners: Utilize event listeners to sync on-chain state changes to your application state dynamically.

State Persistence: Consider state management libraries that can help maintain a reliable state based on current on-chain data.

Best Practices for Debugging

1. Leverage TypeScript's Strong Typing

Be diligent about defining types and interfaces. Type checking will catch many errors at compile time, avoiding runtime failures.

2. Consistent Logging

Implement detailed logging throughout your application. Use a consistent logging strategy to capture errors, transaction details, and state transitions, aiding in tracking down issues later.

3. Utilize Development Tools

Tools like Truffle, Hardhat, and debugging options within IDEs (e.g., Visual Studio Code) can assist in capturing more complex issues. Use features like step-through debugging to inspect state at various execution points.

4. Write Tests

Always ensure your blockchain applications are covered by unit tests and end-to-end tests. Use frameworks such as Mocha, Chai, or Jest. Testing can help identify issues before they become problematic in production.

5. Read Documentation

Given the rapid evolution of blockchain technologies, ensure you're up to date with the latest libraries and frameworks' documentation. Understanding breaking changes and standard practices can save time debugging in the long run.

Debugging TypeScript-based blockchain applications can be challenging, yet understanding common issues and implementing effective debugging strategies can significantly reduce development friction. By leveraging TypeScript's features, maintaining clear and concise logs, and writing comprehensive tests, developers can build more reliable blockchain applications and enjoy a more efficient development process.

Chapter 11: Implementing Smart Contract Security with TypeScript

This chapter delves into leveraging TypeScript to enhance the security of smart contracts, focusing on both theoretical principles and practical applications. By combining TypeScript's safety features with established smart contract security best practices, developers can create more robust blockchain applications.

11.1 Understanding Smart Contract Security

Smart contracts are self-executing contracts with the terms of the agreement directly written into code. While their automation and transparency offer revolutionary benefits, they are also susceptible to various vulnerabilities. Common threats include reentrancy attacks, overflow/underflow errors, and access control issues. Addressing these vulnerabilities is essential to building trust, especially in financial applications.

11.1.1 Common Smart Contract Vulnerabilities

Reentrancy Attacks: Occurs when a contract calls an external contract that in turn calls back into the original contract, potentially manipulating its state unexpectedly.

Arithmetic Errors: Issues stemming from poorly managed math operations, especially in languages that do not safeguard against integer overflow and underflow.

Access Control Flaws: Weaknesses that allow unauthorized users to execute sensitive operations or alter vital data.

11.2 Why TypeScript?

TypeScript, a superset of JavaScript, adds static typing to the language, enabling developers to catch errors during compile time rather than runtime. This feature is particularly valuable for smart contract development, where errors can lead to irreversible consequences. The use of TypeScript coupled with design patterns can significantly improve the reliability of smart contracts.

11.2.1 Type Safety and Its Principle

Type safety ensures that operations in a program do not produce type errors, which can lead to unexpected behaviors. By utilizing TypeScript's strong typing system, developers can ensure that only valid types are passed and used within functions, resulting in fewer run-time errors and a clearer understanding of data structures.

11.2.2 Enhancing Readability and Maintainability

TypeScript's syntax helps document code better than traditional JavaScript, making it easier for teams to understand complex smart contracts and maintain them over time. The use of interfaces and types promotes clear definitions of contract structures, improving collaboration among developers.

11.3 Setting Up TypeScript for Smart Contracts

To begin using TypeScript for smart contract development, follow these steps:

Install Node.js and TypeScript: Ensure that Node.js is installed on your machine. Use npm to install TypeScript globally.

```bash
npm install -g typescript
```

Set Up a New Project: Create a new directory for your smart contract project and initialize it with npm.

```bash
mkdir MySmartContract cd MySmartContract npm init -y
```

Install Required Libraries: Depending on the blockchain platform, you will need to install libraries such as ethers.js or web3.js along with TypeScript definitions.

```bash
npm install ethers
npm install --save-dev @types/node
```

Create a `tsconfig.json` File: This file will manage TypeScript settings and compiler options.

```json
{
"compilerOptions": { "target": "ES6", "module": "commonjs", "outDir": "./dist", "strict": true, "esModuleInterop": true, "skipLibCheck": true
},
"include": ["src/**/*"], "exclude": ["node_modules"]
}
```

```
```

11.4 Building a Secure Smart Contract in TypeScript

To illustrate secure smart contract practices using TypeScript, we will implement a simple ERC20 token contract with built-in security measures.

11.4.1 Token Contract Example

Here's a simplified version of an ERC20 token contract, showcasing key security features.

```typescript
import { ethers } from "ethers";

// Define a simple interface for an ERC20 Token interface ERC20 {

totalSupply(): Promise<number>; balanceOf(owner: string): Promise<number>;

transfer(recipient: string, amount: number): Promise<boolean>;

}

// SecureERC20 implements the ERC20 interface class SecureERC20 implements ERC20 {

private balances: Map<string, number> = new Map();
private totalSupplyValue: number = 0;

constructor(initialSupply: number)          {
this.totalSupplyValue = initialSupply;

this.balances.set("owner", initialSupply); // Assign total supply to the owner

}
```

```
async totalSupply(): Promise<number> { return
this.totalSupplyValue;
}
async balanceOf(owner: string): Promise<number> {
return this.balances.get(owner) || 0; // Default to 0 if no
balance
}
async transfer(recipient: string, amount: number):
Promise<boolean> {
const sender = "owner"; // Usually, you'd use an address
from the transaction context if (amount <= 0 || amount >
(await this.balanceOf(sender))) {
throw new Error("Invalid transfer amount");
}
this.balances.set(sender, (await this.balanceOf(sender)) -
amount);          this.balances.set(recipient,          (await
this.balanceOf(recipient)) + amount); return true;
}
}
```
` ` `

11.4.2 Security Practices

Access Control: Ensure that sensitive functions have
appropriate access control checks.

Input Validation: Validate inputs to prevent
erroneous actions, such as negative transfers or exceeding
balances.

Event Logging: Emit events to log transfers and important actions, allowing better tracking on the blockchain.

11.5 Testing and Auditing

No smart contract is secure without thorough testing. Using TypeScript's type system aids in creating reliable tests. Frameworks like Hardhat or Truffle can be utilized to run tests. Implement unit tests to validate every function, particularly focusing on edge cases associated with security vulnerabilities.

11.5.1 Mocking and Stubbing

Mock external contract interactions to test how your contract behaves under various scenarios. For instance, simulate a malicious contract attempting reentrancy on your token transfer function.

11.5.2 Automated Security Audits

Explore tools such as Slither or MythX, which can automatically analyze smart contracts for security vulnerabilities. While these tools should not replace manual audits, they can significantly aid in identifying potential flaws.

By embracing TypeScript and the principles outlined in this chapter, you can significantly increase the security of your smart contracts and contribute to a safer blockchain ecosystem.

Common Smart Contract Vulnerabilities and How to Avoid Them

This chapter explores common vulnerabilities, their real-world implications, and strategies to avoid them using TypeScript frameworks.

1. Reentrancy ### Description

Reentrancy is one of the most notorious vulnerabilities found in smart contracts. It occurs when a contract calls another contract and allows the second contract to call back into the first contract before the initial execution is complete. This can lead to unexpected changes in contract state or unauthorized fund transfers.

Example

In the infamous DAO hack, the vulnerability in recursive calls allowed attackers to drain the contract's funds. ### Prevention Strategies

Use the Checks-Effects-Interactions Pattern: Always check conditions and update the state of the contract before interacting with external contracts.

```typescript
function withdraw(uint256 _amount) public {
require(balances[msg.sender] >= _amount, "Insufficient balance"); balances[msg.sender] -= _amount; // Effects
payable(msg.sender).transfer(_amount); // Interaction
}
```

Use Mutexes: Implement a reentrancy guard to prevent multiple calls to the same function.

```typescript
bool private locked;

modifier noReentrancy() { require(!locked, "No reentrant calls"); locked = true;

_;

locked = false;

}
```

2. Integer Overflow and Underflow ### Description

Integer overflow and underflow occur when arithmetic operations exceed the bounds of the integer type. In many cases, the result wraps around, leading to unintended behaviors like negative balances or excessive values.

Example

An attack could occur by exploiting this vulnerability to manipulate token balances or contract states. ### Prevention Strategies

Use SafeMath Library: Leverage libraries like OpenZeppelin's SafeMath for basic arithmetic operations to handle overflow and underflow.

```typescript
import { SafeMath } from "@openzeppelin/contracts/utils/math/SafeMath";

function increaseBalance(uint256 amount) public {
balance = SafeMath.add(balance, amount);

}
```

```
```

Use Solidity 0.8 or Later: As of Solidity version 0.8, overflow and underflow checks are included by default, making it more secure against these issues.

3. Gas Limit and Loops ### Description

Depending on the implementation, a smart contract function executing loops may run into gas limit issues. If a transaction exceeds the gas limit, it fails, potentially causing loss of funds or incomplete operations.

Example

If a loop iterates over a dynamic array to transfer tokens, it may be limited by the block gas limit. ### Prevention Strategies

Avoid Unbounded Loops: Design functions that avoid complex loops or that process elements in smaller batches.

```typescript
function batchTransfer(address[] calldata recipients,
uint256 amount) external { require(recipients.length <=
MAX_BATCH_SIZE, "Exceeds batch size"); for (uint256 i
= 0; i < recipients.length; i++) {

// Transfer logic

}

}
```

Implement Off-Chain Processing: Move heavy computations off-chain and use off-chain solutions if possible.

4. Timestamp Dependence ### Description

Smart contracts that depend on block timestamps can be manipulated by miners. Miners can control the timestamps slightly, which can lead to vulnerabilities when time-based logic is implemented.

Example

A contract could be set to execute actions based on the block timestamp, which miners could target for their advantage.

Prevention Strategies

Avoid Using Now/Block Timestamps for Critical Logic: Instead, use block numbers or state transitions for critical processes.

```typescript
require(block.number >= someBlockNumber, "Block number too low");
```

Use Timers Judiciously: Incorporate time-based actions sparingly and understand the risks involved. ## 5. Improper Access Control

Description

Access control issues arise when functions meant for restricted access can be called by unauthorized users. This oversight can lead to critical vulnerabilities where sensitive operations are accessible to anyone.

Example

A common mistake is forgetting to restrict access to

functions that should be limited to only the owner of a contract.

Prevention Strategies

Use Role-Based Access Control: Implement modifiers to restrict function calls based on roles.

```typescript
modifier onlyOwner() {
require(msg.sender == owner, "Not the contract owner");
_;
}
function sensitiveFunction() external onlyOwner {
// Function logic
}
```

Audit and Review Access Control Logic: Regularly review your access control setup to ensure that sensitive functions cannot be accessed without the proper prerequisites.

Understanding common smart contract vulnerabilities is essential for developing secure blockchain applications. By following strategies such as employing design patterns, utilizing established libraries like OpenZeppelin, and implementing thorough testing and access control measures, developers can significantly reduce the risks associated with smart contract development.

Using TypeScript to Strengthen Security in Blockchain Applications

TypeScript, a statically typed superset of JavaScript, offers tools and techniques that can significantly enhance the security of blockchain applications. This chapter will explore how TypeScript can be leveraged to bolster security, minimize vulnerabilities, and promote best practices in blockchain development.

Understanding the Security Landscape of Blockchain

Before delving into the merits of TypeScript, it's essential to understand the common security threats that blockchain applications face. These risks include:

Smart Contract Vulnerabilities: Issues such as reentrancy, integer overflow/underflow, and improper access control can compromise smart contracts, leading to financial losses.

User Input Validation: Insufficient validation can result in injection attacks or unintended consequences when users interact with the blockchain.

State Manipulation: Attackers may manipulate the state of a blockchain application, making it critical to safeguard against malicious attempts.

Developers must implement safeguards to mitigate these risks, and TypeScript can act as a valuable ally in this endeavor.

Benefits of TypeScript for Security ### 1. Static Typing

One of TypeScript's most significant advantages is its static typing feature. This allows developers to define data types explicitly, which helps catch type-related errors during the development phase rather than at runtime. By enforcing type checks, TypeScript enables developers to:

Identify potential vulnerabilities early in the development lifecycle.

Reduce the likelihood of unexpected behaviors caused by incorrect assumptions about data types.

Improve the clarity and maintainability of code by providing clear contracts for function inputs and outputs.
2. Enhanced Tooling and IDE Support

TypeScript benefits from robust tooling and IDE support, which can greatly enhance developer productivity and code safety. Features such as intellisense, automatic code completion, and real-time error highlighting help developers write more secure code by:

Providing immediate feedback on coding errors and potential vulnerabilities.

Offering suggestions for best practices and code improvements.

Simplifying the process of navigation and understanding large codebases, which is particularly valuable in intricate blockchain applications.

3. Improved Code Clarity and Maintainability

Strongly-typed languages promote better code clarity, which is essential for detecting and addressing security issues. In a blockchain context, where contracts can handle substantial amounts of value, maintainability is crucial. TypeScript encourages developers to write clear and self-documenting code, allowing teams to:

Easily identify and rectify security issues.

Facilitate code reviews and audits by providing clearer insight into contract logic.

Enable onboarding of new developers who may need to work with complex smart contracts. ### 4. Interfaces and Type Definitions

TypeScript's ability to define interfaces and custom types allows developers to create more secure APIs. By using interfaces to enforce contracts between different components of a blockchain application, developers can ensure:

Consistency in data structures, minimizing the risk of errors stemming from incorrect data formats.

Safer interactions between smart contracts and front-end UIs, as type mismatches will be caught at compile-time.

Better documentation of APIs, improving security through clarity and understanding of how components should interact.

Practical Implementation: Securing a Smart Contract

To illustrate the principles mentioned above, let's consider a simplified example of a smart contract written in TypeScript using the Hardhat framework, which enables developers to easily create, test, and deploy Ethereum-based smart contracts.

Example: A Simple Token Contract

```typescript
import { Contract, Signer } from "ethers";

interface Token {

balanceOf(address:        string):        Promise<number>;
```

```
transfer(to: string, amount: number): Promise<boolean>;
}
```

```
class SimpleToken implements Token { private balances:
Map<string, number>;
```

```
constructor() {
```

```
this.balances = new Map<string, number>();
```

```
}
```

```
balanceOf(address: string): Promise<number> {
```

```
return Promise.resolve(this.balances.get(address) || 0);
```

```
}
```

```
async   transfer(to:   string,   amount:   number):
Promise<boolean> {
```

```
// Input validation: Ensuring amount is a positive value if
(amount <= 0) {
```

```
throw new Error("Transfer amount must be greater than
zero.");
```

```
}
```

```
const senderBalance = await this.balanceOf(to); if
(senderBalance < amount) {
```

```
throw new Error("Insufficient balance.");
```

```
}
```

```
// Logic to perform the transfer (omitted for brevity)
this.balances.set(to, senderBalance - amount); return
true;
```

```
}
}
```
` ` `

Security Considerations in the Example

Type Safety: By using TypeScript, we define an interface `Token` that ensures any implementation adheres to a specific structure, reducing the chance of unexpected behaviors.

Input Validation: The `transfer` method includes checks on input values, addressing common vulnerabilities related to user input, such as ensuring that the transfer amount is greater than zero and that the sender has sufficient balance.

Error Handling: Using exceptions instead of failing silently or returning incorrect values helps maintain integrity in interactions across the blockchain.

By leveraging static typing, enhanced tooling, better code clarity, and interfaces, developers can proactively address potential vulnerabilities, leading to more resilient blockchain applications.

Conclusion

As we reach the end of our journey through "TypeScript for Blockchain: Unlock the Full Potential of TypeScript in Web3 Development," it's clear that the fusion of TypeScript and blockchain technology presents a transformative opportunity for developers and businesses

193

alike. Throughout this book, we have explored the diverse applications of TypeScript in the Web3 landscape, from smart contract development to decentralized application (dApp) creation.

TypeScript's strong typing, enhanced tooling, and improved maintainability empower developers to construct robust and scalable blockchain solutions. The ability to catch errors early in the development process and the seamless integration with modern JavaScript frameworks make TypeScript an invaluable asset in the rapidly evolving world of decentralized technologies.

As Web3 continues to grow, the demand for secure, efficient, and user-friendly applications will only increase. By leveraging TypeScript's full potential, developers can build systems that are not only functional but also uphold the core values of decentralization and transparency that are fundamental to blockchain technology.

We encourage you to take the insights and skills you've gained from this book and apply them to your own projects. Whether you're embarking on a new venture or enhancing existing applications, embracing TypeScript can lead to higher productivity and more reliable codebases.

As you navigate the challenges and innovations of Web3 development, remember that community engagement is key. The blockchain ecosystem thrives on collaboration, and sharing knowledge is essential for collective growth. Join forums, participate in discussions, and contribute to open-source projects to stay at the forefront of this dynamic field.

Thank you for choosing "TypeScript for Blockchain." We

hope this book has equipped you with the knowledge and confidence to harness the power of TypeScript in your blockchain endeavors. The future is bright for developers committed to pushing the boundaries of what's possible in Web3, and we look forward to seeing the incredible applications you will create. Happy coding!

Biography

Adrian is a passionate innovator and a visionary in the world of **Miller**, blending deep expertise with a relentless drive to push boundaries. With a background rooted in **web development, TypeScript programming, and blockchain technology**, Adrian thrives at the intersection of cutting-edge technology and practical applications. His work in **web applications** has empowered countless developers and entrepreneurs to build scalable, high-performance digital solutions.

Beyond his technical prowess, Adrian is fueled by a love for problem-solving and creative innovation. Whether he's architecting blockchain solutions or refining his latest **TypeScript-powered application**, his mission is always the same—to simplify the complex and unlock new possibilities for others.

When he's not coding or writing, you'll find Adrian exploring the ever-evolving landscape of decentralized technology, mentoring aspiring developers, or experimenting with the latest web frameworks. His dedication to learning and sharing knowledge makes his work not just insightful but transformative.

Through this eBook, Adrian brings his expertise, passion,

and real-world experience to guide readers on their own journey—offering not just knowledge, but a roadmap to success.

Glossary: TypeScript for Blockchain

A

API (Application Programming Interface)

A set of rules and protocols that allow different software entities to communicate. In blockchain, APIs facilitate interactions between dApps, smart contracts, and blockchain nodes.

Async/Await

Syntactic sugar built into TypeScript (and JavaScript) that simplifies the use of promises, allowing for asynchronous code to be written in a more synchronous fashion. This feature is particularly useful when interacting with blockchain networks and their respective APIs.

B

Blockchain

A distributed ledger technology that records transactions across multiple computers in such a way that the registered data cannot be altered retroactively. This technology underpins cryptocurrencies and various decentralized applications.

dApp (Decentralized Application)

An application that runs on a decentralized network, utilizing smart contracts and blockchain to operate without a central authority. TypeScript can be used to build the front-end and back-end components of dApps.

EVM (Ethereum Virtual Machine)

The runtime environment for executing smart contracts on the Ethereum blockchain, the EVM is crucial for dApp development on Ethereum. TypeScript can interact with the EVM through libraries like ethers.js or web3.js.

C

Compiler

A tool that converts TypeScript code (with its extended syntax) into JavaScript, which can then be executed in any browser or JavaScript environment. Understanding the compiler's role helps developers in properly configuring their TypeScript projects for blockchain applications.

Contract

In the context of blockchain, a contract usually refers to a smart contract—self-executing contracts with the terms of the agreement directly written into code. TypeScript can be employed to interact with these contracts seamlessly.

D

Decentralization

The process of distributing and dispersing authority, control, or responsibility away from a central authority. Blockchain's decentralization is crucial for security, transparency, and trust in applications.

Smart Contract

A set of code that automatically executes when predetermined conditions are met. Smart contracts are deployed on blockchain networks and can handle transactions, agreements, and even complex computations.

E

Ethereum

A decentralized platform that enables developers to build and deploy smart contracts and dApps. It is one of the most popular choices for blockchain developers using TypeScript.

Event

In blockchain and smart contracts, an event is a logging mechanism that allows contracts to signal that a particular action has occurred. TypeScript can be used to listen and respond to these events within an application.

F

Fork

A change or modification in blockchain software that results in two versions of the same blockchain. A hard fork is typically not backward compatible, while a soft fork maintains compatibility with the previous version.

Front-end

The part of a dApp that users interact with, typically involving the user interface and user experience design. TypeScript can enhance the development of dynamic, interactive front-end applications for blockchain projects.

G

Gas

A unit of measure in Ethereum that quantifies the computational effort required to execute operations, such as transactions and smart contract invocations. Understanding gas fees is essential for developers to optimize dApp performance.

Grayscale

Referring to the representation of cryptocurrency prices or values over time, helping developers and analysts evaluate market trends and make informed decisions during development.

H

Hash

A function that converts an input (or 'message') into a fixed-size string of bytes. Hashing is fundamental in blockchain technology, providing security and integrity by ensuring that data has not been altered.

Hyperledger

An open-source blockchain framework that enables collaborative development of blockchain applications. With TypeScript, developers can create applications that run on Hyperledger networks.

I

Immutable

Referring to the unchangeable nature of data on the blockchain. Once a transaction is recorded, it cannot be altered or deleted, ensuring data integrity.

Infura

A blockchain infrastructure platform that provides developers with easy access to the Ethereum blockchain without needing to run their own nodes. TypeScript can facilitate integration with Infura's APIs for dApp development.

J

JSON-RPC

A protocol that allows remote procedure calls using JSON (JavaScript Object Notation). Many blockchain implementations, including Ethereum, use JSON-RPC to facilitate communication between clients and nodes.

L

Ledger

A record-keeping system that maintains the integrity and order of transactions. In the context of blockchain, each node maintains a copy of the ledger, ensuring that all transactions are verified and replicated across the network.

M

Metamask

A browser extension and mobile app that acts as a cryptocurrency wallet and interface to interact with Ethereum-based dApps. TypeScript developers can integrate Metamask to manage user accounts and transactions.

Node

A computer that participates in a blockchain network. Nodes validate transactions, maintain a copy of the ledger, and propagate transaction information to other nodes in the network.

S

Solidity

A programming language specifically designed for writing smart contracts on the Ethereum blockchain. TypeScript is often used alongside Solidity to develop front-end applications that interact with these contracts.

Testing Framework

A set of tools and libraries that facilitate the development and execution of tests. For TypeScript-based blockchain applications, frameworks like Mocha, Chai, and Jest can ensure the reliability and functionality of code.

T

Token

A digital asset created on a blockchain, usually representing an asset or utility within a dApp. TypeScript can be utilized to develop token standards, like ERC-20 and ERC-721, for unique use cases.

U

User Interface (UI)

The graphical layout and design elements that users interact with in an application. TypeScript enhances UI development through its type safety and tooling support.

W

Wallet

A software application or hardware device that stores private and public keys, allowing users to send, receive, and manage their cryptocurrencies. TypeScript can be used to create interfaces for cryptocurrency wallets.

Web3

Refers to the decentralized web enabled by blockchain technologies. Web3 applications allow users to interact with blockchain networks without intermediaries, and TypeScript is increasingly used to build these applications.

www.ingramcontent.com/pod-product-compliance
Lightning Source LLC
Chambersburg PA
CBHW070945050326
40689CB00014B/3355